Authored and Published by:

**PAUL FREDERICK DWYER**

*Take Another Look, Examining Popular Teaching on the End Times*
By Paul Frederick Dwyer







ISBN: 979-8-9947452-0-5
Library of Congress Cataloging-in-Publication data has been applied for.

Printed in the United States of America
1st Printing

Cover and inside design by: SpeakU Creative

Where and/or how to order bulk copies

# CONTENTS

# INTRODUCTION

YOU MIGHT BE thinking with some reservation, "Oh great, another book on Bible prophecy and the second coming." And I really wouldn't blame you. Why do I think that I, or anybody else, can add anything meaningful to the discussion with the controversy surrounding this subject? The amount of books I've seen in just my lifetime could fill up a bookcase. Some of them have some good insight and commentary, but a surprising number of them hold to some very popular thinking that pervades the land today, only to end up being refuted by a closer examination.

I don't have any axe to grind, and what either you or I believe about the second coming will not speed up Jesus' return or delay it. Neither is it required for us to accurately interpret it to experience salvation. However, what you believe about it could be influencing your life much deeper than you realize, and its impact will either help you or hurt you in planning for the near future. As we will see, a lot of the answers that could address people's fears are being conveniently left out because bad news sells faster than good news. God forbid that anybody's teaching would need to be adjusted!

I'm not attempting to answer everyone's questions. (Nobody else seems to be either.) I am saying that more questions need to be asked, because a lot of the popular answers leave a lot of commas and confusion. It seems they ignore a lot of our past Christian history since Christ appeared the first time. The most popular system of seeing Bible prophecy fulfilled has failed so many times that many are growing deaf to the absolute reality that Christ will appear a second time.

There are reasons for this, and I'd like to encourage you to turn again to the same scriptures and ask yourself: Am I hearing and seeing this clearly? What am I overlooking? It just might benefit you greatly and rekindle a better hope.

# 1

# WHO ARE YOU LOOKING FOR?

*"The woman said, "I know that Messiah" called Christ is coming. When he comes, he will explain everything to us." John 4:25*

## PAST EXPECTATIONS—WHEN CHRIST APPEARED THE FIRST TIME

**IF YOU HAD** lived during the time of the Old Testament (OT) prophecies about Christ's first coming, you would have found yourself embracing a number of pieces that were all part of a large prophetic puzzle. These pieces had been given at numerous times during the development of OT history. The true prophets of God had been faithful to proclaim the prophetic parts given to them individually, but they were vastly different when compared to one another. None of the pieces formed a clear picture of Christ until they all came together when He was actually born and lived.

However, that didn't keep people from predicting what the Messiah would be like and forming their expectations of him.

> *"As to this salvation, the prophets who prophesied of the grace that would come to you made careful search and inquiry, seeking to know what person and time the Spirit of Christ within them was indicating as He predicted the sufferings of Christ and the glories to follow. ..."*
> *I Pet. 1:10–11*

Depending on what you desired in the Messiah may have influenced the kind of Messiah you were expecting and looking for. How he might appear may have been difficult to comprehend, but when He would appear was clearly stated by the promise given thru the prophet Daniel in 538 B.C. This is known as the 70 weeks prophecy and it forms a divine timeline that directs the people's expectations as to when the Messiah would appear the first time. We'll look at it closely later, but for the moment understand that this was a very accurate signpost for the nation of Israel to focus on.

Obviously, there were the angelic announcements the night Christ was born, and the testimony of the shepherds. This was followed by the prophetic confirmations of Simeon and the prophetess, Anna, at the dedication of Jesus as a young infant. *(Luke 2:8–38)* At that moment, we're told that Anna "*... continued to speak of Him to all those who were looking for the redemption of Jerusalem." Luke 2:38*

As time went on, the ground of people's hearts was watered by the highly effective ministry of John the Baptist. This helped prepare the way as the people's hearts were tenderized and softened up by the rugged prophets preaching. Expectations were running high, and more than one person knew the time was close for the public appearance of the Messiah.

> *"Now while the people were in a state of expectation and all were wondering in their hearts about John, as to whether he might be the Christ, John answered and said to them all, "As for me, I baptize you with water; but One is coming who is mightier than I, and I am not fit to untie the thong of His sandals; He will baptize you with the Holy Spirit and fire." Luke 2:15–16*

Here were some commonly held views of Christ when He came the first time.

**A Royal Messiah –** Without a doubt, many of them were looking for the Messiah to be a royal figure from Jerusalem, the city of David. After all, God had promised that a descendant of David's would always rule and that his throne would be established forever. *(II Samuel 7:16)* Nobody could have imagined that the Messiah would come from a small village in Galilee, or that He hung out with tax collectors, and reached out to lepers.

**A Military Messiah –** This was certainly a popular expectation in light of the fact the Jews were subjected to Roman occupation at the time of Christ. Besides, great warriors were part of their history—Joshua, David, Gideon, etc.

**A Prophet who returns** – God had promised Israel through the last of the OT prophets, Malachi, that He would send Elijah before the great and terrible day of the Lord. *(Mal. 4:5)* Several New Testament (NT) passages show that the Jews expected Elijah himself to personally reappear. But Jesus pointed out to his disciples that this was fulfilled through the ministry of John the Baptist. John came in the spirit of Elijah to turn the hearts of people in expectation of the Messiah's arrival *(See Matt. 11:11–14)*

**A suffering Servant** – Isaiah had prophesied a suffering Messiah, but this was not a popular expectation, or one easily understood. How could the Messiah be "cut off" and save the nation? *(Isaiah 53)* Anybody hung on a tree (the cross) was considered under a curse. *(Gal. 3:13)*

**A Human Messiah** – Most Jews expected the Messiah to be human only, not divine. God living among them in a human bodily form *(John 1:11,14; Col. 2:9)* was challenging, and one of the reasons the Pharisees attacked Christ was due to His equality with the Father. *(John 5:18)*

As an example of how three completely different prophecies concerning Christ all came to pass; consider the following from the second chapter of the gospel of Matthew. Wise men show up from the east and start inquiring where the King of the Jews had been born. The religious leaders tell Herod that the town was to be Bethlehem, according to the OT prophet Micah. *(Micah 5:2)* Sure enough, that's where Christ was born.

Matthew then referenced Hosea 11:1 which said, "Out of

Egypt have I called my Son." The angels warned Joseph to flee to Egypt because Herod would try to kill baby Jesus. Joseph was later told to return from Egypt after the death of Herod, and then, the young family settled in the town of Nazareth fulfilling the prophecy that Christ would be a Nazarene.

Before their fulfillment, these prophecies seemed contradictory on their own, but completely understood when history unfolded. We need to remember this when it comes to seeing how our current prophetic era unfolds. ***If people misunderstood how Christ would come the first time, do you think it's possible they will do the same with His second coming?***

## PRESENT EXPECTATIONS—WHEN CHRIST APPEARS THE SECOND TIME

Some of our expectations are correctly formed and some are not. Some are the result of good scholarship and some are the result of faulty teaching. Sometimes old thinking dies a slow death, regardless of the truth that confronts it. As I think you'll see, many of the commonly held views about the second coming and the conditions preceding it, really need to be re-examined, and if necessary, discarded for our own good.

Regardless of how we may interpret his coming, we better believe that He will return!

> *"So Christ was sacrificed once to take away the sins of many; and he will appear a second time, not to bear sin, but to bring salvation to those who are waiting for him."*
> *Hebs. 9:28*

# 2

# WHEN JESUS RETURNS— PROMISES MADE, PROMISES KEPT

**ONE DAY IN** the near future, the Author of eternal life, the finisher of our faith will return to this earth. He stated repeatedly that he would return. He wants to return. I want Him to return. We need Him to return!

After Christ had been raised from the dead, He commissioned his apostles to carry the gospel message to the ends of the earth. In the book of Acts we see a connection between His first coming and His second coming.

> *"They were looking intently up into the sky as he was going, when suddenly two men dressed in white stood beside them. "Men of Galilee," they said, "why do you stand here looking into the sky?* ***This same Jesus*** *who has been taken from you into heaven, will come back in* ***the same way*** *you have seen him go into heaven." Acts 1:10–11*

For those who are ready and looking forward to His second coming, His return will be the most glorious event of their whole entire lives. It will be the fulfillment of their deepest desires and greater than their wildest dreams.

> *"For the Lord himself will come down from heaven, with a loud command, with the voice of the archangel and with the trumpet call of God, and the dead in Christ will rise first. After that, we who are still alive and are left will be caught up together with them in the clouds to meet the Lord in the air. And so we will be with the Lord forever. Therefore encourage each other with these words."*
> *I Thess. 4:16–18*

But for those who are not ready and have mocked the idea of His return with cynical laughter and disobedient lives, His return will be the worst nightmare they can possibly think of. A horror movie gone really bad, and one that doesn't appear to have an end.

Again, writing to the church at Thessalonica, Paul called it "pay back" time.

> *"God is just: He will pay back trouble to those who trouble you … This will happen when the Lord Jesus is revealed from heaven in blazing fire with his powerful angels. He will punish those who do not know God and do not obey the gospel of our Lord Jesus. They will be punished with everlasting destruction and shut out from the presence of the Lord and from the majesty of His power on the day he comes to be glorified in his holy people and to*

*be marveled at among all those who have believed. This includes you, because you believed our testimony to you.*
*II Thess. 1:6–10*

Wherever you stand on the subject at the moment, you can be sure of this:

***It will happen!*** A million demons cannot stop it, and a thousand atheists will not be able to explain it away. His second coming will be sudden and apparent to all. His appearance will be visible. It will be unexpected. It will be worldwide.

We would do well to pay attention to the words of Jesus. He has quite a track record. It's been said that there are approx. 333 prophecies that pertain to the first coming of Christ, and that there are approx.154 promises of His second coming. Jesus faithfully fulfilled all those prophecies of his first coming, and the words that He spoke about his second coming are being fulfilled around us everyday.

Jesus knew the secrets of men's hearts—*John 2:25*

Jesus knew personal details of people and their deepest needs—*John 4:13–29*

Jesus knew what the future held for those close to him—*John 21:17–19*

Jesus knew the tribulation that his own generation would face—*Luke 21:20–24*

Jesus accurately predicted the events of history that have played out over the past 2,000 years.—*Luke 17:22–30; Matt. 24:3–39*

> Jesus knows what is going to happen on the planet earth and He has told us in advance what to prepare for and how to prepare for it.—*Luke 21:34–36*

That's a prophetic record that the psychics, the mediums, the horoscopes and all the gossip magazines cannot match! It's incredible that on the basis of that alone more people are not paying attention to his words.

With what I've stated up to this point, you would find a consistent amount of agreement among ministers, churches, and Bible prophecy teachers. But *how* we get to the second coming and *what* takes place before that is filled with many opinions and interpretations as we shall see. It's surprising that with such a lack of clarity on so many issues surrounding Christ's coming that many in the church are quite rigid in their positions. *(Yes, I realize I take that risk as well.)*

## AN INCONVENIENT TRUTH

Part of the challenge lies in the fact that the ever-changing landscape of world history and geopolitical issues makes it hard to interpret the future with much accuracy. Perhaps that's a misplaced focus that we've pushed too far.

There are actually at least four major views among the church world in regard to Bible prophecy, with some variations inside a couple of those views. Some have been around a long time, and others are more recent, and in some circles more popular. There are many godly people who hold to these views and they should be respected for their efforts to make sense of it all.

Although, I would like to point out that too many preachers, teachers, and authors are conveniently withholding the other views for fear it may expose the shortcomings of their own views, or fears of denominational constraints. Perhaps they've just not considered it in an honest and open mind. I fell prey to this as a young believer and student in ministry. For the first eight years of my Christian walk, everything that I read, everything that I was taught, and everything that I taught others, was all from one dominant view. I was completely unaware that there was any other view.

It literally took a short, but profound "aha moment" in my life to begin to see that I had read into the scriptures something that was not really there. From that point on, my little ship of prophecy turned around and began to sail a different course. It was not long after that, I learned that my views were not held by me alone, but were actually embraced by many others.

It's not the intent of this book to try to defend or examine in detail everything about Bible prophecy, the second coming, or the message of Revelation. Having said that, I think some views have serious weaknesses because of a misplaced focus, and perhaps the best thing we can do is not to answer every question and objection, but to redirect our focus and call attention to what is being overlooked.

## GOD'S SECRET IS GREATER THAN YOUR REVELATION

*"The secret things belong to the Lord our God, but the things revealed belong to us and our children forever ..." Deut. 29:29*

*"No one knows about that day or hour, not even the angels in heaven, nor the Son, but only the Father. As in the days of Noah, so it will be at the coming of the Son of Man. For in the days before the flood, people were eating and drinking, marrying and giving in marriage, up to the day Noah entered the ark; and they knew nothing about what would happen until the flood came and took them all away. That is how it will be at the coming of the Son of Man." Matt. 24:36–39*

I believe in revelation. I've received revelation from God's word many times. I've had revelations about myself, about my family, about others, and to a small degree revelation about the near future. We should actually experience that because Jesus promised us that this would happen when the Holy Spirit comes into our life. *(See John 16:13)*

But one revelation God has never given me is the day or hour when Jesus will return. And guess what? *He has not given that revelation ever to anybody on the planet earth!* Not your favorite TV Evangelist, not your denomination, or a popular author.

If He did, He would be violating His own word and that's not going to happen.

Everybody's personal revelation is subject to the word of God. That is the supreme counsel that will stand the test of time. Everybody that claims they know the day or hour of Jesus' return has always failed to match the date correctly. And there's a reason for that, which I will cover shortly.

I remember when I was a young man in my 20's and I was attending a church in the small town where I lived. There was an older man in his mid 80's at the time. He was a genuine believer that really loved the Lord and loved others. He was quite convinced that the Lord had shown him that he would not pass away until the Lord had returned. I thought to myself, "Jesus had better come quick, because that brother will be pushing a hundred soon!"

Of course, he meant well, but what had motivated him was a passage of scripture that applied to a man named Simeon and how it pertained to the first coming of Christ. *(See Luke 2:25–26)* Here we see that the Holy Spirit had revealed to Simeon that he would not pass away until He had seen the Lord's Christ, which was fulfilled when he saw Jesus as a baby.

Another thought along this line is when senior believers sometimes make the statement that they feel the Lord's return is very soon, even in their own lifetime. It's an honest impression, but most of the time it doesn't mean they are trying to set a date, it means they are returning to the Lord. In other words, they are recognizing that their work is done soon and they will be going home to the Lord.

Sometimes I'm asked if I believe this is the last generation, to which I reply,

"It is for you!" You don't get a second chance. Reincarnation is not a biblical doctrine, or a true teaching. What we do in this life is what gets rewarded in eternity.

> *"If the master returns and finds that the servant has done a good job, there will be a reward. I tell you the truth, the master will put that servant in charge of all that he owns. But what if the servant is evil and thinks, 'My master*

*won't be back for a while,' …*

*… The master will return unannounced and unexpected, …" Matt. 24:46–50 NLT*

*The reason the servant is described as good, is not because he knew the day or the hour of his master's return, but because he was obeying his master's orders in light of what he did not know. We would do well to follow that example.*

Let's look into what Jesus told us we *could* know and what we *would* not know.

# 3

# SIGNS AT THE END OF THE AGE, OR SIGNS IN EVERY AGE?

## WHAT THE SIGNS SAY AND WHAT THEY DON'T SAY

ONE DAY SHORTLY before He went to the cross, Jesus had just finished an intense time of preaching in the city of Jerusalem. Like any group from a small town, the disciples were impressed by the big city features of Jerusalem; especially Herod's temple that had taken almost 50 years to build.

In OT prophetic fashion, Jesus declared that the temple would be completely leveled. Being good Jewish men, the disciples were naturally concerned for their nation, so they asked Jesus when the temple would be torn down.

> *"Tell us", they said, "**when** will this happen, and **what** will be **the sign** of your coming and of the end of the age?" Matt. 24:3*

Along with the first question, they asked him two other

questions. They naturally assumed that the destruction of the temple had to be involved with his return, and the end of the age, or the world as they knew it. They could not have imagined that the temple would face destruction without that including an end to the world. They knew the world was bigger than Israel, but it's easy to see that they had the same kind of narrow-mindedness that we would have for our own home country.

What follows through the rest of the chapter is Jesus answering all three of their questions, without establishing any specific dates, or drawing boundaries around any particular group of people throughout the time of world history. His answer prepared the disciples and the early church to face the trouble that *their* generation saw, but also included *all generations* since that time.

> *"Watch out that no one deceives you. For many will come in my name, claiming, 'I am the Messiah', and will deceive many. You will hear of wars and rumors of wars, but see to it that you are not alarmed. Such things must happen, but the end is still to come." Matt. 24:4–6*

He did not say, "Try to predict the hour or day of my return based on what you see."

He went on to say that there would be conflict among nations, earthquakes, famines, persecutions, various kinds of social unrest, and the preaching of the gospel in the whole world. (*Matt. 24:7–14*)

Jesus does not want you to be misled or deceived. Trouble has come, and more trouble is coming, but all of these signs are not the end of the world. For sure, it may be the end of *somebody's* world, but it's not the end of *the entire world*. If the distress is great enough through various wars, famines, and upheaval, then *somebody's* world may end, but *not* the entire world.

This is why it's so difficult to set dates for the Lord's return because the signs are not intended to predict that. Unfortunately, too many people are misled by this, and many people drift into date setting by a misplaced focus on current world events.

If the signs that Jesus mentioned were all that was necessary to fulfill and predict his return, then he would have already returned a long time ago. As a matter of fact, the same signs and features that precede his coming were all manifested in the first century before the end of the book of Acts—every one of them!

These general signs are cyclical and they will happen every century and generation. It just seems like there are more of them because you hear about them immediately with today's media technology, and the fact that the chaos is increasing due to the growth of the world's population.

Jesus said no man knows the hour or the day. *(Matt. 24:36)* Every observable event has to be interpreted in the light of this statement. The return of Christ cannot be determined by the *frequencies* of any event, or the *magnitude* of any event, or the *location* of any event. And yet, people keep trying.

## WHAT GOES AROUND, COMES AROUND

**A simple review of the many catastrophes during the past 2000 years** of world history will show a far greater loss of life than many events today. Again, they may have been the end of *somebody's* world, but not the end of the whole world, or this present age. Consider the following:

**The deadliest wars** – Hands down, the two deadliest wars in human history have been WWI with 15–22 million deaths, followed by WW2 with an estimated 50–85 million deaths. Most people thought Jesus would have returned after that. There has rarely been a year without some kind of war for thousands of years.

**The biggest earthquakes** – Looking at two websites that have studied and compiled the biggest earthquakes, eight of the ten biggest earthquakes all happened over 100 years ago. The largest was in China in 1556, with a loss of 830,000 lives. In the modern era, the Sumatra earthquake of December 2004 comes to mind.. The quake measured 9.2, with a loss of over 200K lives. [Note 1] [Note 2]

Modern equipment is capable of recording these events with a greater precision, so it may seem as if they've increased, when in reality, they probably have not.

**The deadliest diseases & pestilence** – The bubonic plague from 1334–1353 took out over one quarter of the population of Europe. The great influenza pandemic of 1918 wiped out 50 million people—one fifth of the world's population was attacked by the virus. It is said that tuberculosis has been the deadliest disease in history causing the death of 1 billion people!

**The most severe famines** – Between 108 B.C. and

1911 A.D. there have been 1,828 recorded famines. The Great Chinese Famine of 1959–1961 is estimated to have caused the death of 30–50 million people, largely the results of Mao Zedong's failed policies.

## WHY ALL OF THIS SHOULD MATTER TO YOU

This by no means an exhaustive list. My point is, that in each of these events Jesus did not return, but *somebody's* world ended. When we forget this, hope and faith for the future are crushed and disillusion sets in. People stop planning and building and start preparing for the worst, however, Jesus said, *"see to it you are not alarmed. Such things must happen, but the end is still to come." Matt. 24:6*

When the disciples asked Jesus about the destruction of Jerusalem and the end of the world, His first statement was, *"watch out that no one deceives you. For many will come in my name, claiming, I am the Christ, and will deceive many." Matt. 24:4–5*

When we lack discernment and good understanding about any subject, we can be misled into error and fall captive by the words of influential people—even those who have come in the name of the Lord.

We would do well to be a good bit suspicious and unemotional when it comes to predictions with worldwide impact and consequences. Scripture directs us to, *"test everything and hold on to the good." I Thess. 5:21*

When the message we hear and believe is taken out of the full biblical context, we can fall prey to influencers and compromise the fullness of what God has for us in the future. The 1970's and the 1980's saw its share of people influenced by "date setters" who thought they had it all figured out. The extreme side of this saw people quitting their jobs, running up credit cards, not paying house payments, and in general, a negative approach to any future planning.

The capstone of this prophetic blindness was seen in the book, "88 reasons why Christ will come in 1988." Uh, hello? We're still waiting! When the iron curtain came down in 1989 a lot of popular predictions got overturned and provoked a re-interpretation. The date setting problem has actually happened several times over the past 150 years, so a caution against it bears repeating.

## THE FOLLY OF DATE SETTING—SOME EXAMPLES

As early as the second century, false prophets were suggesting dates for the return of Christ. Montanus, a new convert to Christianity believed himself to be the anointed prophet of God. Two women joined him and claimed to be the mouthpiece of the Holy Spirit. All of their predictions failed.

In the fourth century, a man named Donatus commanded attention when he stressed that only 144,000 people would be chosen by God. He found this magic figure in Rev, 14:1, the same verse the Jehovah's witnesses use to proclaim their own version of this heresy.

As the last day of 999 approached, "the old basilica of St. Peter's at Rome was thronged with a mass of weeping and trembling worshippers awaiting the end of the world," believing that they were on the eve of the millennium. Lands, homes, and household goods were given to the poor as a final act of contrition to absolve the hopeless from the sins of a lifetime. Some Europeans sold their goods before traveling to Israel to await the second coming of Christ. This mistaken application of Bible prophecy happened again in 1100, 1200, and 1245.

William Miller, the father of the modern Seventh Day Adventist denomination, proclaimed October 22, 1844 as the return of Christ based on his calculations. 100K of his disciples gave away their possessions in the lead-up. When it failed to come to pass, it was renamed the "Great Disappointment". For sure.

The biggest selling book on Bible prophecy was the "Late Great Planet Earth", published in 1970. While admittedly a wake up call to the condition of world societies, it miscalculated the return of Christ by stating emphatically, it would come to pass within the generation that saw the rebirth of the nation of Israel in 1948—a period of 40 years.

Finally, a minister named Harold Camping, tried several times to predict the coming of Christ through numerical calculations he was convinced were in the Bible. The last prediction I heard about was May 21, 2011, which was actually splashed on a big billboard right up the street from my house at the time.

I don't doubt the sincerity of many of the "date setters". It's a classic example of how we can be sincere, and sincerely wrong. What is surprising is how frequently they try to overthrow the clear words of Christ and press for a different agenda. I'm sure when Jesus made the statement that nobody would know the hour or the day, He took into account all the cutesy ways that men try to simplify it, and reduce it down to mathematical calculations and chasing storms.

Even post resurrection, the first disciples had a lingering concern about the future of their first century world. Displaying the same narrow-mindedness, they asked Jesus, "... *Lord, are you at this time going to restore the kingdom to Israel?"*

He said to them, *"It is not for you to know the times or dates the Father has set by His own authority. But you shall receive power when the Holy Spirit comes on you, and you will be my witnesses in Jerusalem, ..." Acts 1:6–8*

In other words, "Get out there and get something done."

# 4

# WHEN ARE THE LAST DAYS?—WHAT IS THE CORRECT VIEW?

**B**EFORE WE CONTINUE on, I'd like to take a moment and qualify when are the last days. In hearing what some people say, they'd have you believe that the last days are still future, or the last days only began during the difficult time period we are currently in.

**There are four NT passages that speak clearly about the term, "last days".**

*"… but in these last days he has spoken to us by his Son, whom he appointed heir of all things, …" Hebs. 1:2*

*"He was chosen before the creation of the world, but he was revealed in these last times for your sake." I Pet. 1:20*

*"But mark this: There will be terrible times in the last days." II Tim. 3:1*

> *"In the last days, God says, I will pour out my Spirit on all people, your sons and daughters will prophesy, . . . " Acts 2:17*

So, it seems obvious that the NT writers saw themselves living in the last days already, in the first century after the resurrection of Christ. "Last days" is a term to express a period of time that was separate from the former days, or the OT period. The ministry, death and resurrection of Christ initiated a completely new period of time that Paul called a *"dispensation (or age) of grace". (Eph. 3:3–9)*

God's grace and the goodness of God is being offered to all generations and this is the drawing card that leads people to repentance. *(Rom. 2:4)* Peter confirms the same thing when he says, *"The Lord is not slow in keeping his promise, as some understand slowness. He is patient with you, not wanting anyone to perish, but everyone to come to repentance." II Pet. 3:9*

Have you noticed, not everybody is happy with the message of grace. In these last days, Paul said terrible times will come and history has shown that for the past 2,000 years God's offer of grace is being extended to each generation. Some like it, some don't—some receive it, some won't. Aren't you glad God was patient with you?

Future judgment will be so painful because present grace is so amazing in its offer.

Peter already faced "grace rejecters" because he was already living in the last days.

> *"First of all, you must understand that in the last days scoffers will come, scoffing and following their own evil*

*desires. They will say, "Where is this 'coming' he promised? Ever since our fathers died, everything goes on as it has since the beginning of creation." II Pet. 3:3–4*

Did you catch that? "*Everything goes on as it has ...*"

Sometimes people say, "Well, you know brother, we're living in the last of the last days." You don't know that—and neither does anybody else!

The true last days have lasted over 2,000 years already and there is no way to clearly predict the end of this age of grace and God's offer of salvation. Remember, the terrible times of the last days are not a clear predictor of Christ's return. They're a clear directive on why we need a strong authentic relationship with God.

Again, is this the last generation? It is for you and me. Only time will tell how many more generations will follow.

## THE FOUR MAJOR VIEWS OF BIBLE PROPHECY

It may come as a surprise to many readers that more than one viewpoint exists in regards to *how* the last days will come to pass. It came as a surprise to me. I discovered that authors and teachers had a way of conveniently hiding the other views, and droning on and on with their interpretation of the end times, no matter how ridiculous some of it sounds.

Many of these views are people simply parroting what they've picked up from the schools they went to, and it underscores how quickly we can become rigid in our thinking. How badly we need the Holy Spirit's help to catch what He is saying to us!

I know, I've been there. I can also say that I was open to being adjusted and it's my prayer that you'll consider that too.

The apostle Paul said that we see in part and we know in part, and when it comes to complete fulfillment of God's worldwide plan some things just cannot be seen clearly until the hour of their fulfillment—we only see it partially by spiritual insight, or a prophetic image like in the book of Revelation. Some events are quite obvious when you review the history of the church, so there is no arguing with that.

It's not my goal to fully explain the four major views in this book. I've defined them here with simple statements and I'll try to amplify the differences as I go forward, and direct you to other material in the appendix at the end of the book. [Note 1]

**The Past View –** It all happened in the first century

**The Historic View –** It happened some time in the past history of the church

**The Future View –** It all happens in a future literal seven year period

**The Present View –** What has happened is still happening

# 5

# THIS GENERATION OR THAT GENERATION?

**HISTORY HAS BEEN** aptly expressed as *His*-story—God's plan for the salvation of man. NT Christianity is essentially a historical religion in the sense that it's not based on poetry, fantasy, or philosophy. It's a record of real people, expressing a real faith by their words and actions. Today, we have a history of what their lives looked like.

The historical outgrowth of the first believers and the early church is seen in the book of Acts. Here, the essential structure of the church begins and patterns are developed that we see the modern church using to this day.

All of us should have a general understanding of the church's history, because if you don't know what has been experienced by the church in its history, then there's no way to accurately determine where it is, or where it may be going.

Doctor Luke can be trusted—here's what he said: "… *since I myself have carefully investigated everything from the beginning, it seemed good also to me to write an orderly account for you,*

*Theophilus, so that you may know the certainty of the things you have been taught." Luke 1:3–4*

Luke continues with the same accuracy in writing the book of Acts. *(Acts 1:1)*

World history and archeology has determined that Luke is very reliable in recording his historical accounts. Likewise, Luke has shown that the world history of his time was also reliable. In other words, they actually confirm one another.

You'll see why this is important in just a bit.

Remember, in chapter 3, I pointed out that the disciples specific question was ***when*** will the temple be torn down? But they tied that together with another question: *"**what** will be the sign of your coming and of the end of the age?" Matt. 24:3*

What follows is Jesus answering both of their questions without regard to specific dates or times. He covers what I call, "the big picture". *(Matt. 24:4–14)*

He covers a large, unknown period of time, and sums it up by saying, *"this gospel of the kingdom will be preached in the whole world as a testimony to all nations and then the end will come." Matt. 24:14*

After preparing them to recognize the many cycles of world tribulation, He returns to their first question which was specifically about their nation, the nation of Israel.

## THIS IS THAT

Jesus was under no illusion to the spiritual condition of the nation of Israel during his ministry. The religious structure and leadership were rotten to the core. I can just imagine the intensity of his scathing rebuke of the religious leaders in Matt. 23. No miracle he ever performed was good enough for them—no sign was evidence enough.

If you follow the many passages in the gospels, you will note a consistent theme about the condition of Israel at the time of Christ. Consider these:

> *"To what can I compare* ***this generation?*** *They are like children sitting in the marketplaces and calling out to others: 'We played the flute for you, and you did not dance; we sang a dirge and you did not mourn.' Matt. 11:16–17*

In other words, Jesus is saying, "nothing I ever say or do will change your mind".

To the hypocritical leaders of that generation Jesus had this to say:

> *"And so upon you will come all the righteous blood that has been shed on earth, from the blood of righteous Abel to the blood of Zechariah son of Berekiah, whom you murdered between the temple and the altar. I tell you the truth, all this will come upon* ***this generation.****"*
> *Matt. 23:35–36*

> *"The men of Nineveh will stand up at the judgment with* ***this generation*** *and condemn it; for they repented at the preaching of Jonah, and now one greater than Jonah is here. The queen of the South will rise at the judgment with* ***this generation*** *and condemn it; ..." Matt. 12:41–42*

Jesus described the nation as unable to maintain it's deliverance by saying:

> *"And the final condition of that man is worse than the first. That is how it will be with* ***this wicked generation.****" Matt. 12:45*

> *"For the Son of Man in his day will be like the lightning, which flashes and lights up the sky from one end to the other. But first he must suffer many things and be rejected by* ***this generation****." Luke 17:34–35*

These statements by Jesus show us that he separated ***that generation*** from any others yet future. Everything he said about the tribulation Israel would face in the first century referred to ***that generation***, not one some time in the future.

This seems to be one of the glaring oversights of the future view. In the future view, the tribulation that Israel has already faced in the first century gets placed in some seven year period in the future. Past history would beg to differ.

*"I tell you the truth,* ***this generation*** *will certainly not pass away until all these things have happened." Matt. 24:34*

Let me say it again this way: ***This generation*** that Jesus was talking about, is ***that generation*** that experienced great tribulation in the first century.

Can you begin to see that?

Let's see what Jesus said would happen and if there's a record of it in history.

## A SPECIFIC SIGN FOR A SPECIFIC GENERATION

The first indication of a coming calamity is foretold by Jesus the day he rode into town on a new donkey.

> *"As he approached Jerusalem and saw the city, he wept over it and said, … The days will come upon you when your enemies will build an embankment against you and encircle you and hem you in on every side. They will dash you to the ground, you and the children within your walls. They will not leave one stone on another, because you did not recognize the time of God's coming to you."*
> *Luke 19:41–43*

Specifically, the sign that applied to ***this*** generation, or ***that*** generation, was the destruction of the temple. In Matt. 24:15 Jesus called it, "the abomination of desolation", but Luke's account amplifies it much more.

> *"**When you see** Jerusalem being surrounded by armies, you will know that its desolation is near. Then let those who are in Judea **flee to the mountains**, let those in the city get out, and let those in the country not enter the city. For this is the time of punishment in fulfillment of all that has been written.*
>
> *How dreadful it will be in those days for pregnant women and nursing mothers! There will be great distress in the land and wrath against this people.*

> *They will fall by the sword and will be taken as prisoners to all the nations. Jerusalem will be trampled on by the Gentiles until the times of the Gentiles are fulfilled."*
> *Luke 21:20–24.*

The generation that first heard those words saw them fulfilled within the first 40 years of Jesus making that statement. Jesus said, *"**this generation** will certainly not pass away until all these things have happened. "Matt. 24:34*

## WHAT TEMPLE WAS JESUS REFERRING TO?

The disciples asked when the temple that *they saw* in *their generation* would be torn down and destroyed. Jesus answered their question straight forward and gave them and the early church an unmistakable sign—armies surrounding the city. To refer to any other kind of temple would not have answered the disciple's primary question.

The future view commonly holds that the "abomination of desolation" *(Matt. 24:15)* will be some kind of idol placed in the holy of holies in a rebuilt temple in the future.

Jesus was talking about the temple in His generation, and the generation the disciples lived in. Anything else would not have prepared them, or the early church which resided there!

I'll deal with the question about a rebuilt temple in a later chapter, but it should be evident that people have read into this passage something that is not taught in context at all.

## WHEN YOU SEE, THEN YOU FLEE

This is an interesting statement with a profound warning. If the early church was *in the city* when it was surrounded on the *outside*, then how could they flee to the mountains? Clearly, Jesus wanted His people, the early church, to be warned, but how would that work its way out?

Much of what we know about first century Israel, and that period of history comes from the Jewish historian, Josephus. He had been a soldier against the Romans early on. He eventually surrendered to the Romans and tried to get the Jewish nation to come to agreeable terms with the Romans.

His writings of the history of the Jewish nation are clearly tied closely to the OT Scriptures, and his writings about the NT period are available and considered quite reliable. Josephus records that the nation as a whole ignored several unusual supernatural signs in the years before its destruction. By 66 A.D., the nation of Israel slid into open defiance of the Roman occupation, and over the next four years Roman armies tightened their grip on the rebellious nation.

Josephus says, one of Caesar's worst procurators, Floris, assumed control of Judea, and did things which brought the Jews into violent rebellion—more than he could handle. He was replaced by Cestius Gallus who marched his armies into Israel and subdued a number of towns as he advanced toward Jerusalem.

Soon, Jerusalem was surrounded by Roman armies and the early church knew they must flee. But how could they when the city was surrounded?

Cestius and his armies had so much early success that the Jews were ready to give up and surrender. If they would have opened up the gates, the city and the temple would be saved. But Jesus had prophesied that it would be destroyed. Josephus says, "without any reason in the world"—Cestius withdrew his troops and suddenly departed! This filled the Jews with renewed courage and they pursued the retreating army, inflicting heavy losses. [Note 1]

Surely the early church must have seen this as the hand of God, and the chance to immediately pack up and leave.

As it turned out, there was a brief interval of time before the armies would return and destroy the city. Eusebius, the historian of the early church, states that all the genuine believers in Christ departed Jerusalem, and went to Pella and other places beyond the Jordan river. Not one of them perished in the destruction of Jerusalem. Jesus had given them a clear sign of escape and they did! [Note 2]

Nero had Cestius replaced with Vespasian, who ordered his son, Titus, to go to Alexandria and bring the 5th and 10th legions from Egypt to subdue the violence in Judea. However, a crisis interrupted those plans, (probably Nero's death), and Vespasian returned to Rome where he became the new emperor in 70 A.D.

In 70 A.D. Titus, the Roman general, surrounded the city of Jerusalem during the feast of unleavened bread when the city was filled with many visitors.

Once the Roman armies surrounded the city, nobody was able to escape. The population was reduced by starvation, infighting among the city's inhabitants, and crucifixion by the Roman soldiers, among other things.

The temple was completely destroyed and over 1.1 million people lost their lives in the invasion. 97,000 survivors were taken captive into surrounding nations and became slaves. From his vantage point, Josephus declared that "the multitude of those who perished exceeded all the destruction that either men or God ever brought upon the world." Note 3 The full history is more brutal than this!

The city that Jesus had wept over sadly missed their day of visitation, and the greatest light that God had ever sent them, Jesus, had correctly prophesied that severe judgment would take them by surprise. Notice how closely Christ's words compare to the history that took place:

*"... There will be great distress in the land and wrath against this people. They will fall by the sword and will be taken as prisoners to all the nations. Jerusalem will be trampled on by the Gentiles ..." Luke 21:23–24*

If there ever was a generation that saw a time of fulfilled signs that indicated Jesus return, then surely it was the first century church. And yet, Jesus did not return at that time. We shouldn't be surprised that He didn't, because He told them that the end was not yet, even though it was a time of chaotic change for ***that*** generation, and clearly it was the end of the city of Jerusalem at that time.

You can try to reinterpret the history, but you can't change what really happened. If Jesus had not spoken correctly in regard to his own generation, then it would leave doubts in our minds about whether we could trust Him about our future.

But he did speak correctly and it all came to pass. We can trust our future to play out how He said it would, even if others are bent on trying to sell us the wrong interpretation!

## IF YOU DON'T KNOW—YOU DON'T GO

When you set aside the "future view" interpretation it seems obvious that Jesus had two different groups in mind—specifically the apostles generation and the first century church, and then all other generations *whenever* they live in history.

The apostle's generation was given a specific sign, and in essence Jesus was telling them, when you ***see***, then you ***flee!***

Since that time, all other generations that make up the church are called to continue to preach the good news, make disciples, plant and build for the future, because we don't know the hour or day of His return.

So, if you ***don't know***, you ***don't go!***

Remember, when the disciples asked Jesus about the destruction of the temple, they wrongly assumed that it would include the end of the age and Christ's return. But it did not.

Following are some **key differences** between what the first century church in Jerusalem saw, compared to what the church has seen since that time.

1. When you ***see*** Jerusalem surrounded by armies, then you ***flee*** *Luke 21:20–21* Israel will be trampled under foot by the Gentiles, (as in, "closed down"), but the gospel will be preached to all nations, … (as in, "opened up") *Matt. 24:14*

2. The ***generation that sees*** the destruction of Jerusalem would not pass away until all things take place. *Luke 21:32* Here, Jesus clearly put a time stamp on the destruction of the temple. Within 40 years of His prophecy it came to pass, "*… these things must take place first, but **the end***

***does not follow immediately***. … *Nation will rise against nation, and kingdom against kingdom, … " Luke 21:9–10* Clearly, the destruction of the temple and Jerusalem brought it to an end at that time, however, it's obvious that wars and conflict have continued through history.

3. There ***was time*** to flee before Jerusalem was destroyed. *Luke 21:21* There is ***no time*** to flee when Christ returns. *Matt. 24:36, 42, 44*

4. The sign that Jerusalem would be destroyed was armies surrounding the city. *Luke 21:20* The sign that Christ has returned will be His visible, personal appearance, which will be a complete surprise. *Matt. 24:30–31*

5. The early church knew when the time of Jerusalem's destruction would come. *Luke 21:20–24, 32*—They were actually told to leave their post at that time. Occupying our post is the most obvious position when we don't know the hour of His return. *Matt. 24:44–46 When you see, then you flee—When you don't know, you don't go!*

6. When Jerusalem was destroyed in 70 A.D., the remaining Jews were *scattered* to other nations. *Luke 21:24* When Christ returns a second time He will *gather* his elect (Jew & Gentile), from every corner of the earth. *Matt. 24:30–31*

## WHAT WAS THEN, IS STILL HAPPENING NOW

As I said earlier, you can try to reinterpret Christ's prophetic words, but it's impossible to ignore the plain history that has already come to pass. Many prophecies that people are waiting to see fulfilled have already been fulfilled!

Israel might have achieved independent statehood beginning in 1948, but the Gentile nations continue to try to trample upon it.

Likewise, the countless cycles of upheaval in the world are not enough to determine the end of our generation. There's a certain sense of normality that will continue right up till the time of Christ's return. Consider *Luke 17:26–30*

> *"Just as it was in the days of Noah, so also will it be in the days of the Son of Man. People were eating, drinking, marrying up to the day that Noah entered the ark. Then the flood came and destroyed them all. It was the same in the days of Lot. People were eating and drinking, buying and selling, planting and building. … It will be just like this the day the Son of Man is revealed."*

No man knows the hour or the day when everything looks like its, "just another day". Nobody is expecting His return when society is functioning in some kind of capacity that it always has. Peter confirms this is the same stance that the scoffers and mockers take because everything looks largely the same.

> *"Above all, you must understand that in the last days scoffers will come, scoffing and following their own evil desires. They will say,, "Where is this 'coming' he promised? Ever since our ancestors died, everything goes on as it has since the beginning of creation."* ***II Pet. 3:3–4***

# 6

# A REBUILT TEMPLE, OR A REBUILT PEOPLE? PART I

**IF THERE'S ANYTHING** that seems unnecessary for the completion of God's plan, the idea that a third temple needs to be rebuilt with a return to some kind of sacrificial system has got to rank up there near the top.

In this chapter I want to consider these kinds of questions: Is there enough evidence in Scripture to support a literal temple being rebuilt in Israel? And if so, why would this be necessary in light of the great sacrifice of Christ over 2K years ago? Is it possible that this teaching has actually misled people into thinking that it's a Spirit led plan, when in reality it's simply a popular and misguided idea?

## THE SHODDY FOUNDATIONS FOR A REBUILT TEMPLE

Where does this idea come from? It lies at the center of the future-view teaching, which teaches that a period of great tribulation is kicked off with the rapture of Christians, and followed by a period of seven literal years. During this seven-year period some kind of antichrist leader enters into a covenant of sorts with the nation of Israel, and in the middle of this seven-year period he will put a stop to their offerings and turn against the nation of Israel. In other words, he defiles their temple which was rebuilt to prepare their offerings to the Lord. This is a major part of the future-view teaching on the end times.

The problem with this view is that it's complete fiction. Far too many ministers have put together a hodgepodge of scriptures and presented them with some slick presentations that sound convincing, but are rarely examined. Most ministers graduate from their Bible schools and simply pick up the system of prophecy they were instructed in, and away they go. Just keep repeating it long enough and loud enough, and most people will be convinced, even if it's total error.

## MORE SHOCKING STATEMENTS

There is nothing stated or implied anywhere in the NT that a temple will be rebuilt. In fact, there's every reason to believe that the season for temples has passed and the Lord is not into temples anymore. And while I'm pointing that out, I might as well tell you that there is no passage in the entire NT that teaches a literal seven year tribulation period—not one!

Usually when I say that, it's followed by the same thing I hear now—silence, not even crickets! Surprisingly, the roots of this teaching starts by taking just one verse completely out of context, but when you examine many other scriptures it quickly appears out of place.

The verse that is used is the very last verse of **Daniel 9** which says:

> *"He will confirm a covenant with many for one seven. In the middle of the seven he will put an end to sacrifice and offering. And on a wing of the temple, he will set up an abomination, until the end that is decreed is poured out on him." Daniel 9:27*

By adding on other verses from other passages, an erroneous "house of cards" is built which is nothing like the context teaches. Left on its own, this verse seems fairly complex and confusing. We should naturally start with this question: Who is the "He"that the scripture is referring to? You certainly need the full context of the chapter to determine who the "He" is. Depending on who you think the "He" is, that will guide your understanding on what "He" came to do.

## WHO IS THE FOCUS OF DANIEL'S 70 WEEKS?
### *A BRIEF HISTORY*

Approximately 539 B.C., and about the 66th year of Israel's captivity, the prophet Daniel is seeking God through prayer and fasting, desiring to know the outcome of their captivity. The 70 years of desolation was almost complete and the Lord had directed what His people should do at that time. See *Daniel 9:2–20 and Jeremiah 29:10–14*

Daniel is praying about the completion of 70 years of captivity, and specifically about the nation of Israel and the city of Jerusalem. The angel Gabriel appears and tells him about 70 'sevens'—or a total of the next 490 years! *(Each 'seven' was a period of seven actual years.) Daniel got much more than he asked for. See Daniel 9:20–24.*

Focusing on the rest of the 9th chapter, *Daniel 9:24–27*, it should be obvious that the "He" of the context is referring to the Anointed Ruler and what He will do. This can only find fulfillment in the work of Christ, as Israel's promised Messiah. What did He come to do?

## THE ANOINTED RULER'S "JOB DESCRIPTION"

Starting with Daniel 9:24, and interpreting that in the light of what Christ came to do, you can begin to see how the vision and prophecy of the 70 weeks was completed, and opened up a new dispensation and age for mankind. Consider the following seven points:

1. ***490 years are decreed for your people and the holy city***
   Clearly, the Lord was in no hurry. He would use Cyrus to permit Israel to return to their homeland and the city would be rebuilt with streets and a trench, but it would be rebuilt in times of trouble. *v. 9:25* In the time of Nehemiah, they actually labored with a trowel in one hand and a sword in the other. *(See Nehemiah 4)*

   From the going forth of the commandment to restore and rebuild Jerusalem until the Anointed One appeared, 483 years would come to pass.

Eventually the promised Messiah would appear, and some that were in tune with the Spirit, and followed the history of the prophecy could pretty much pinpoint when He would show up. Consider Simeon, Anna, and John the Baptist—*Luke 2:25–38; Matt.11:10*

2. ***To finish the transgression …***
   Christ offered a wisdom greater than Solomon, and more preaching power than Jonah, but the nation's leadership was bent on rejecting Christ as the promised Messiah. As I mentioned in a previous chapter this was the greatest transgression they could commit, and it left them defined as, "more wicked", than the previous generations. *(Matt. 12:45)*

3. ***To put an end to sin***
   John the Baptist had declared that Jesus is *"the Lamb of God who takes away the sin of the world" John 1:29.* The death of Christ is the one perfect sacrifice that put an end to sin. Here, the message of the book of Hebrews shines brightly.

   *"For Christ did not enter a man-made sanctuary that was only copy of the true one; He entered heaven itself, now to appear for us in God's presence. But now he has appeared once for all at the end of the ages to do away with sin by the sacrifice of himself. So Christ was sacrificed once to take away the sins of many people; and he will appear a second time, not to bear sin, but to bring salvation to those who are waiting for him." Hebs. 9:24, 26, 28*

4. ***To atone for wickedness***
(Make atonement for iniquity) *"We all, like sheep, have gone astray, each of us has turned to his own way; but the Lord has laid on him the iniquity of us all. Is. 53:6*

*"But now he has reconciled you by Christ's physical body through death to present you holy in his sight, without blemish and free from accusation". Col. 1:22*

5. ***To bring in everlasting righteousness***
Again, so many passages of the NT makes this abundantly clear. Only the person and the work of Christ alone can establish a lasting righteousness for us. *"because by one sacrifice he has made perfect forever those who are being made holy." Hebs. 10:14*

*"This righteousness from God comes through faith in Jesus Christ to all who believe. … and are justified freely by his grace through the redemption that came by Christ Jesus." Rom. 3:22, 24*

*"Since they (Israel) did not know the righteousness that comes from God and sought to establish their own, they did not submit to God's righteousness. Christ is the end of the law so that there may be righteousness for everyone who believes." Rom. 10:3–4*

6. ***To seal up vision and prophecy***
Christ "sealed" OT prophecy by fulfilling what was

written of him. He stated of himself: *"On him God the Father has placed his seal of approval." John 6:27*

He told his disciples after his resurrection:

*Luke 24:44: "This is what I told you while I was still with you: Everything must be Fulfilled that is written about me in the Law of Moses, the Prophets, and the Psalms."*

The early church was convinced the focus was on Christ and what he came to do.

*"But this is how God fulfilled what he had foretold through all the prophets, saying that his Christ would suffer,"*

*"Indeed, all the prophets from Samuel on, as many as have spoken have foretold these days. And you are heirs of the prophets and of the covenant God made with your fathers." Acts 3:18, 24–25*

7. ***To anoint the Most Holy***
   Even though Christ is the Truth, and spoke nothing but the truth, He did not rely on his own testimony to be the only witness. *(John. 5:31; 8:14)* As you read about the life and ministry of Christ, you recognize that there are at least nine different witnesses testifying that he is the Most Holy. Even the demons recognized who he really was *(Mark 1:24)*.

Peter sums up the ministry of Christ beautifully when He recalls in Acts 10:38: *"how God anointed Jesus of Nazareth with the Holy Spirit and power, and how he went around doing good and healing all who were under the power of the devil, because God was with him." Acts 10:38*

This is what the angel Gabriel told Daniel that the Anointed Ruler, (Christ), would do when he came to the nation of Israel and the city of Jerusalem.

## WHEN WOULD THIS ANOINTED RULER APPEAR ?

From the commandment to restore and rebuild Jerusalem until the Anointed One, the ruler, comes would be a total of 483 years. *(Daniel 9:25)*

This was fulfilled during the years from 457 B.C. to 27 A.D. [Note 1]

At the end of this 69 weeks (483 years), Jesus begins his public ministry shortly after being baptized and returning in the power of the Spirit. *Luke 3:22–23; 4:1–4*

Jesus started his public ministry as the long-awaited Messiah at the *beginning* of the 70th and last week of the 70 x 7 prophecy. He ministered for three and a half years, because John mentions four different passovers in his gospel during that time. This also confirms what the prophecy said, that after the 69 weeks the Anointed One would be cut off and have nothing. *(Daniel 9:26)*

## THE CONDITIONS SET BY THE ANOINTED RULER, THE MESSIAH

During the last and final week—the 70th, Jesus called all that would hear his voice, to come into covenant with him, by the blood that he knew he would shed on their behalf. They had to choose Christ—there was no other option for them. Or for us, for that matter.

> *"While they were eating, Jesus took bread, gave thanks and broke it, and gave it to the disciples, saying, "Take and eat; this is my body." Then he took the cup, gave thanks and offered it to them, saying, "Drink from it, all of you. This is my blood of the covenant, which is poured out for the many for the forgiveness of sins. Matt. 26:26–28*

Even stronger covenant terms are seen in this passage:

> *"I tell you the truth, unless you eat of the flesh of the Son of Man and drink his blood you have no life in you. Whoever eats my flesh and drinks my blood has eternal life, and I will raise him up at the last day."*

For those that stayed to truly listen, Jesus said:

> *"The Spirit gives life; the flesh counts for nothing. The words I have spoken to you are spirit and they are life. John 6:53–54; 63*

As the Anointed One, Jesus performed enough miracles for even the most skeptical to believe. But with the nation's leadership it was still never enough. Lazarus being raised from the dead was not convincing enough, even though he had been dead four days.

*"Even after Jesus had done all these miraculous signs in their presence, they still would not believe in him." John 12:37*

*"Yet at the same time many even among the leaders believed in him. But because of the Pharisees they would not confess their faith for fear they would be put out of the synagogue; for they loved the praise from men more than praise from God." John 12:42–43*

## THE MESSIAH DETERMINED THE TIME AND THE OFFERING

Faced with repeated opposition, Christ did not allow anyone to take his life until the appointed time. This had been predetermined by the foreknowledge of God and held in check until the proper time. *(Acts 2:23)*

*"The reason my Father loves me is that I lay down my life–only to take it up again. No one takes it from me, but I lay it down of my own accord. I have authority to lay it down and authority to take it up again. This command I received from my Father. "John 10:17–18*

In the middle of the last and 70th week of the prophecy, he (Christ), put an end to sacrifice and offering by offering up himself for the sins of all people. *Daniel 9:27.*

Here again, the book of Hebrews makes this abundantly clear.

*"Day after day every priest stands and performs his religious duties; again and again he offers the same sacrifices, which can never take away sins. But when this priest had offered for all time one sacrifice for sins, he sat down at the right hand of God." Hebs. 10:11–12*

*"And by that will, we have been made holy through the sacrifice of the body of Jesus Christ once and for all." Hebs. 10:10*

*"Because by one sacrifice he has made perfect forever those who are being made holy." Hebs. 10:14*

The truth of the matter is that Christ brought an end to the sacrificial system by the sacrifice of himself. No other sacrifice is needed by anyone, or for anyone, regardless of Jew or Gentile. The unsaved Jews continued in their blindness operating the sacrificial system until it was destroyed by the Romans with the city in 70 A.D.

You can see the heart of the Father expressed and the will of the Son in *Hebs. 10:8–9*

*"First he said, "Sacrifices and offerings, burnt offerings and sin offerings you did not desire, nor were you pleased with them (although the law required them to be made). Then he said, "Here I am, I have come to do your will." He sets aside the first to establish the second."*

*"By calling this covenant "new", he has made the first*

*one obsolete, and what is obsolete and aging will soon disappear. "Hebs. 8:13.*

And disappear it did!

## CHRIST OPENS UP A NEW WAY TO ENTER GOD'S PRESENCE

When the veil of the temple was torn in two by the power of God at the death of Christ, it signified a new way into the presence of God. All of us can come with confidence to enter the Most Holy Place by the blood of Jesus. *Hebs. 10:19–20*

It is not the will of God for any people, Jew or Gentile, to return to the past sacrificial system. Not in type, shadow, or reality. God is not planning on present day Jews returning to him by focusing on the ashes of the red heifer. He has exalted his Son as the perfect sacrifice and that's where our focus needs to be! The Holy Spirit has come to bear witness of what Christ has done, not what men try to do in the name of the Lord.

Don't you find it odd that with so many orthodox Jews around the world that somebody hasn't tried to build another temple, and reinstitute the sacrificial system in some kind of measure? The NT teaches that we have a better high priest, who offered a better sacrifice by the shedding of his own blood. And now, we have a better covenant based on better promises. *Hebs. 8:6*

What could be better than that? Nothing! Certainly not a return to an old system.

Men in their religious thinking may try to plan on rebuilding a temple, but it shouldn't be promoted and sold as if it's part of God's plan, because it isn't! The world is full of temples and various kinds of sanctuaries that have nothing to do with the true power and plan of God. Even in the far off future God has no plans for his presence to dwell in some kind of literal temple. *(Rev. 21:22)*

## TITUS AND THE ROMAN ARMY IN PROPHECY

Gabriel tells Daniel that after the Messiah is cut off the city and the sanctuary will be destroyed. *Daniel 9:26* In his time, Daniel had no idea how it would all work out in history. However, he had been given a glimpse that many years after him, a very powerful kingdom would arise greater than the others before it, but not greater than the kingdom of God.

Rome was the ruling empire at the time of Christ, and its army led by Titus certainly fulfilled this prophecy by crushing the city and destroying the sanctuary in 70 A.D. This is the abomination of desolation that Jesus warned about in Matt. 24:15. Daniel was living at the end of 70 years of desolation, only to find out that more war and desolations lie ahead during the next 490 years. The city had not been rebuilt since the destruction by the Babylonian armies in 586 B.C., and now Daniel is informed that the city will be rebuilt and destroyed again! It must have been a tough pill for him to swallow.

## THE REMAINING PIECE OF THE 70 WEEKS PROPHECY

When Israel's leadership rejected their Messiah, the Anointed Ruler, Jesus knew that time was growing short, and that heaven's plan was to use the nation's rejection as the opportunity to present his body as the last and final sacrifice for sins. Because of his perfect sacrifice there is no longer a need for the sacrificial system, or for the priesthood of men, or the temple with the most holy place. These were all just a copy of the true sanctuary in heaven. *(Hebs. 9:24)*

The priesthood of men was temporary and looked toward the perfect priesthood of Christ who is our great high priest forever. He does not stand in a literal temple on earth, but in the direct presence of God in heaven.

> *"Therefore, since we have a great high priest who has gone through the heavens, Jesus the Son of God, let us hold firmly to the faith we profess. For we do not have a high priest who is unable to sympathize with our weaknesses, but we have one who has been tempted in every way, just as we are—yet was without sin. Let us then approach the throne of grace with confidence, so that we may receive mercy and find grace to help us in our time of need."*
> *Hebs. 4:14–16*

God is not concerned with getting people into temples today. He's concerned with getting into the human heart—the spirit of man. Wherever people are at, they can find his grace in their time of need through the eternal priesthood of Christ. The earliest believers in the book of Acts, found that God was willing to pour out his Spirit anywhere they gathered—it no longer required a special visit to the temple, or even the local synagogue.

After the death and resurrection of Christ, all that remained of Daniel's revelation of the 70 weeks was three and a half years.

This is fulfilled in two ways, both *natural* and *spiritual.*

**Natural –** Israel's leadership had not received the Lordship of Christ, but the Lord had hundreds of faithful disciples and he confirmed his covenant by pouring out his Spirit upon them first in Jerusalem. As Paul said about the Jews, *"First of all, they have been entrusted with the very words of God." Rom. 3:2*

This pattern seems evident from a number of passages and accounts from Acts.

> *"You will receive power when the Holy Spirit comes on you, and you will be my witnesses in Jerusalem …" Acts 1:8*

> *"Repentance and forgiveness of sins will be preached in his name to all nations, beginning at Jerusalem." Luke 24:47*

> *"When God raised up his servant, he sent him first to you to bless you …" Acts 3:26*

> *"I am not ashamed of the gospel, because it is the power of God for the salvation of everyone who believes: first for the Jew, then for the Gentile." Rom. 1:16*

Although it cannot be proven without a shadow of doubt, it seems reasonable that this first movement to advance the gospel in Jerusalem may well have covered the remaining three and a half years. After all, the 70 weeks prophecy was *"decreed for your people and the holy city"*,—the Jews and Jerusalem. *Daniel 9:24*

It makes absolutely no prophetic sense to establish 69 and

a half weeks concurrently and then separate the last half of week from all the rest by some 2,000 year gap.

**Spiritual –** At least this three and a half year period agrees with the same term used in the book of Revelation. It is used *symbolically* of the entire church age and its not a *literal* period of three and a half years. Once you understand that most numbers in Revelation are used symbolically, (in other words, representing an idea), it becomes easier to understand its message. Only God knows the entire length of the church age period—the rest of us cannot interpret it based on just the things we see.

## A NEW PEOPLE & A NEW TEMPLE

It should not surprise us that the NT gives us permission to apply this time period (three and a half years) spiritually or symbolically. The NT writers freely took terms that applied to natural Israel and applied them to the church, spiritual Israel. God's special people now are Jew and Gentile alike. Writing the letter to the Gentiles in the region of Galatia, Paul said:

> *"There is neither Jew nor Greek, slave nor free, male nor female, for you are all one in Christ Jesus. If you belong to Christ, then are you Abraham's seed, and heirs according to the promise." Gal. 3:28–29*

Paul wrote frequently about how God merged these two groups together and fused them into one new man in Christ.

*"But now in Christ Jesus you who once were far away have been brought near through the blood of Christ. For he himself is our peace, who has made the two one and has destroyed the barrier, the dividing wall of hostility, by abolishing in his flesh the law with its commandments and regulations. His purpose was to create in himself one new man out of the two, thus making peace, and in this one body to reconcile both of them to God through the cross, by which he put to death their hostility.*

*"He came and preached peace to you who were far away and peace to those who were near. For through him we both have access to the Father by one Spirit." Eph. 2:13–18*

Paul clearly says in this NT age of grace, God views his people through the work of Christ and he only sees one group, not two. God is not providing access to different people groups through two different means. All Jews and Gentiles today have to come the same way. There's only one way to access the true presence of God and that's through the Son. *(See John 14:6)*

In the next chapter, we'll see what this means and where our focus should be while living in the end times.

# 7

# A REBUILT TEMPLE, OR A REBUILT PEOPLE? PART II

JESUS WAS SENT as the Messiah to the nation of Israel, but as the Lord of the harvest, and the king of God's kingdom, his vision included more than one tiny nation and one small group of people. We catch a glimpse of this from a statement in John, where Jesus says,

> *"I have other sheep that are not of this sheep pen. I must bring them also. They too will listen to my voice, and there will be one flock and one shepherd." John 10:16*

> *Again, in praying for his disciples, Jesus includes those who would eventually hear the gospel message: "My prayer is not for them alone, I pray also for those who will believe in me through their message that all of them may be one." John 17:20*

Because the nation of Israel as a whole refused to bear lasting fruit, God prepared a new people made up of Jews and Gentiles that recognize Christ alone as the only rightful heir to the throne. Jesus didn't mince any words when he taught the parable of the tenants. He knew he was the stone the builders would reject, but God would use it to bring about change. *(Matt. 21:33–42)*

Jesus finished the parable by saying:

> *"Therefore I tell you the kingdom of God will be taken away from you and given to a people who will produce its fruit. He who falls on this stone will be broken to pieces, but he on whom it falls will be crushed." When the chief priests and the Pharisees heard Jesus' parables, they knew he was talking about them. Matt. 21:43–45*

## PENTECOST AND THE INVITATION TO NATIONS

Starting in the book of Acts, God begins shocking everybody by pouring out his grace and power in a grand fashion at an international gathering called the feast of Pentecost. The spiritual pump was primed by a large prayer meeting that included the original disciples, the mother of Jesus and her friends, and even Jesus' brothers all joined in. Eventually, the group grew to about 120. *(Acts 1:13–15)*

This would make a nice, tidy club of friends to enjoy the blessings of God among themselves, without things getting out of hand. Or so they may have thought. God planned things on a larger scale and beginning with Pentecost he showed that he could speak the language of any group, and he didn't need anybody's permission to do so! *(Acts 2:7–12)*

The original 12 may have even thought that the day of Pentecost was somewhat of a fulfillment of Acts 1:8—*"that they would be witnesses to the ends of the earth."*

It certainly was a small picture of what God would paint on a much larger canvas.

The move on the day of Pentecost was much easier to digest. After all, those that attended were already Jewish in their backgrounds, or warm to the tenets of Judaism. *(Acts 2:11)*

During the first few years of the early church the focus of the preaching was directed to the Jews in the city of Jerusalem, and whoever might be visiting. God was easing them into the waters of ingathering and helping them to shoulder the new load. *(Acts 6:1–7)* But make no mistake about it, the Lord's fishing net was much more expansive than they imagined.

When a great persecution broke out against the church at Jerusalem, it forced the early preachers to consider other people groups that were nearby. *(Acts 8:1,4)* Jesus had softened the early apostle's outlook about the Samaritans by effectively winning over the citizens of Sychar, and the woman at the well. *(John 4:28–39)* The disciples may have thought, *"Well, after all, the Samaritans are half Jewish and half Gentile—you know, the "black sheep" of the family!"* Jesus said all things were possible … so here we go!

You can see the early church bending and adjusting to all kinds of new people, but these people had a certain "Jewishness" about them that made it a little more palatable. When God initiates a stronger signal to go to the Gentiles it is met with great indifference.

*"So when Peter went up to Jerusalem, the circumcised believers criticized him and said, "You went into the house of uncircumcised men and ate with them." Acts 11:3*

Peter, with a good measure of doubt himself, recalls the vision God gave him three times about not seeing the Gentiles as "unclean", but recognizing that God saw them as capable of being "clean", the same as any Jew. *(Acts 10:28; 11:9)*

Peter arrives at the house of Cornelius, a Roman centurion, and finds a house full of Gentiles that are hungry for the message of Christ and the things of God. Peter quickly realizes that any reservations he had are futile in trying to oppose the power of the Holy Spirit. Defending his actions, he told the critical Jews that:

*"As I began to speak, the Holy Spirit came on them as he had come on us at the beginning. So if God gave them the same gift as he gave us, who believed in the Lord Jesus Christ, who was I to think that I could oppose God?"*

*"When they heard this, they had no further objections and praised God saying, "So then, God has granted even the Gentiles repentance unto life." Acts 11:15,17–18*

This should have been convincing enough, but men's traditions can die a slow death and have a fake life all of their own! Many years after the day of Pentecost, the very first church conference and leadership gathering was convened to determine who could really be saved.

*"Then some of the believers who belonged to the party of the Pharisees stood up and said, "The Gentiles must be circumcised and required to obey the law of Moses." Acts 15:5*

Once more, Peter gets up and repeats what God had told him many years before. God had made a choice, now the Jewish believers needed to make a change. *(Acts 15:7)*

*"God, who knows the heart, showed that he accepted them by giving the Holy Spirit to them, just as he did to us. He made no distinction between us and them, for he purified their hearts by faith." Acts 15:8–9*

Reminding them that the pursuit of the law could not produce sinless perfection, Peter asks these opposers of grace:

*"Now then, why do you try to test God by putting on the necks of the disciples a yoke that neither we nor our fathers have been able to bear? No! We believe it is through the grace of our Lord Jesus that we are saved, just as they are." Acts 15:10–11*

## A NEW PEOPLE WITHOUT AN OLD TEMPLE

Peter recognized this new generation of faith being expressed by the merging of the Jews and Gentiles together. The new focus would be on a spiritual house, not a rebuilt temple.

> *"you also, like living stones, are being built into a spiritual house to be a holy priesthood, offering spiritual sacrifices acceptable to God through Jesus Christ." I Pet. 2:5*

> *"But you are a chosen generation, a holy nation, a people belonging to God, that you may declare the praises of him who called you out of darkness into his wonderful light. Once you were not a people, but now you are the people of God; ..." I Pet. 2:9–10*

As early church history unfolds, it's significant to note that God never told any of his early church leaders, or congregations of Jews and Gentiles, to form some kind of new literal temple to meet in, be it in the city of Jerusalem or anywhere else.

- They were not required to go up to Jerusalem, (when it still stood), and participate in special Jewish festivals, which were merely a shadow of things to come. They were told the true reality was found in Christ, not a building *(Col. 2:16–17)*

- They were not asked to pay a temple tax, or to pay some kind of tithe or special offerings to replace temple stones that may have worn out, or to upgrade the furniture.

- They were not asked to provide livestock animals to keep the sacrificial system going. The idea that the Jewish people will return to some form of a temple and sacrificial system is completely against everything the book of Hebrews and the NT teaches.

God's plan wasn't to preserve the old temple in Jerusalem, no matter how magnificent it may have been. He planned on building a new temple and infusing it with the power and presence of his Holy Spirit. He wasn't planning on getting people in, but rather equipping, maturing, and sending them out into all the world, wherever his Spirit would lead them!

You can tell that the early apostles and preachers caught the spirit of the message and had the new insight—a new day had begun. Stephen was one of the first when he declared,

> *"However, the Most High does not live in houses made by men. As the prophet says: Heaven is my throne and the earth is my footstool. What kind of house will you build for me? says the Lord. Or where will my resting place be? Has not my hand made all these things?" Acts 7:48–50*

To the Athenians, the apostle Paul told them,

> *"The God who made the world and everything in it is the Lord of heaven and earth and does not live in temples built by hands. And he is not served by human hands, as if he needed anything, because he himself gives all men life and breath and everything else." Acts 17:24–25*

## JESUS, THE FORERUNNER OF THE NEW TEMPLE

Jesus initiates this coming change when he first declares to the Jewish leaders:

> *"Destroy this temple, and I will raise it again in three days." The Jews replied, "It has taken 46 years to build this temple, and you're going to raise it in three days?" But the temple he had spoken of was his body. After he was raised from the dead, his disciples recalled what he had said." John 2:19–22*

Luke records that he went to Nazareth where he had been brought up, and went into the synagogue as was his custom. *(Luke 4:16)* But that day his preaching took on a new air, and being handed the scroll of Isaiah,

> *"… Unrolling it, he found the place where it is written: "The Spirit of the Lord is upon me, because he has anointed me …" Luke 4:17–18*

And just to make sure that the congregation did not think he was referring to anybody else, he added, *"Today this scripture is fulfilled in your hearing." Luke 4:21*

In Jesus' day, the religious hierarchy of Pharisees and Sadducees were not fond of reaching out to people, so it's no surprise that most of the miracles Jesus did happened away from the temple and synagogues. Jesus miracles proved he was the son of God, but they were not performed by the fact that he is the Son of God.

Jesus did no miracles of any kind until the anointing of the Holy Spirit came upon him at his baptism. *(Mark 1:9–11; 21–34)* But he didn't keep the mission and the anointing to himself. In brief, let me remind you of the others He sent out with the same authority and anointing.

- The original twelve disciples and apostles—*Mark 6:14–15; John 14:12*
- The seventy others sent out later—*Luke 10:1,17*
- All believers in his name—*Mark 16:15–18*
- All future believers filled with the Holy Spirit—*Acts 1:8; 2:38–39*

The point of all this is that Jesus set into motion a pattern that continues to this present day. The focus is on a new temple filled with the personal presence of God, and empowered by the Holy Spirit—the same Spirit that once filled the Holy Place in the temple.

If this was the direction that Jesus was taking the church, we should expect to see this revealed in the rest of the NT, and in particular, the letters to the churches. And indeed, this is what we find when Paul writes to the churches.

## HOW PAUL USED THE WORD "TEMPLE"

In the NT when Paul uses the word, "temple", he is *never* referring to a literal temple. He is *always* speaking of the *spiritual temple*—which is the individual believer, and the corporate body of Christ—the church.

The Greek word Paul used was, "naos", which meant a temple, or a highly decorated shrine. The Corinthians were accustomed to seeing lots of temples and shrines in their day, so the image that flashed in their minds was probably much grander than what we first think of.

Paul applies the temple truth to us *spiritually*. God has chosen to dwell in the hearts and spirits of his people—an inner sanctuary that has been swept clean by the blood of Jesus, and it's now adorned with his grace and righteousness!

*"Don't you know that* ***you yourselves are God's temple*** *and that God's Spirit lives in you? If anyone destroys God's temple, God will destroy him, for God's temple is sacred, and* ***you are that temple.****" I Cor. 3:16*

*"Do you not know that* ***your body is a temple of the Holy Spirit****, who is in you, whom you have received from God? You are not your own; you were bought at a price." I Cor. 6:19*

*"What agreement is there between the temple of God and idols? For* ***we are the temple of the living God****, as God has said: I will live in them and walk among them, …" II Cor. 6:16*

*"In him (Christ), the whole building is joined together and rises to become a holy temple in the Lord. And in him* ***you too are being built together to become a dwelling in which God lives*** *by his Spirit." Eph. 2:21–22*

As a side note, its common for pastors and ministers to say on any given Sunday, "Isn't it great to be in the presence of God and come together in the house of the Lord." I'm sure they mean well, but the statement is misleading, and it gives the idea to people that they have to come into a building to experience God's presence. It's the people who are holy, not the building! That's been proven over and over again.

As we will see, Paul's use of the word, "temple" has a huge bearing upon the idea of some kind of antichrist figure desiring to sit in a literal temple in the future proclaiming himself as God. Satan has no serious interest in this, because there's no true power in a literal temple made with stones. The church, the body of Christ, carries the real power and that's the real threat to the enemy's camp.

# 8

# A GAME OF MUSICAL CHAIRS

**IN THE SIMPLE** children's game of musical chairs, the set up of the game consists of perhaps six chairs and seven participants. As the music plays, the children walk around the chairs until the music suddenly stops playing. The basic goal is to grab a seat quickly when the music stops. Because there's only six chairs for seven players, somebody won't find a seat and must sit out the rest of the game. Another chair is removed, and now there are only five chairs for six players as the music plays again. The game ends when the music stops playing, and only one of two players grabs the final chair.

In this chapter, let's consider this question: Who's been sitting in the temple?; And who's the winner when the music stops playing?

## PAUL, THE APOSTLE OF THE HEART SET FREE

When you look at God's choice of the apostle Paul from

a natural perspective, it makes no sense. But when you look at it from God's perspective it makes complete sense. God took a young, hot-headed Pharisee bound by legalism, and turned him into a tireless servant filled with a deep understanding of the grace of God for all people.

Paul recognized that his former life showed him to be the worst of sinners, but God had shown him mercy and would use his life as an example of what is possible for others. *(I Tim. 1:15–16)* Paul was also very convinced that God had given him a special grace and deep revelation to impart to the church, convincing them of what it meant to be in Christ, and to have Christ in them, the hope of glory. *(See Eph. 3:2–11)*

## WHAT TEMPLE WAS PAUL CONCERNED ABOUT ?

As I mentioned in the previous chapter, part of Paul's revelation was that God's presence and care was for a new temple—the human spirit, individually, and also collectively as the spiritual body of Christ—the church. *(I Cor. 3:16; 6:19)* Again, every time Paul uses the word,"temple", he is never referring to a literal temple. He is always referring to the spiritual temple—the individual believer and the corporate body of Christ.

This is what Paul, and the rest of the apostles cared about. They knew the literal temple in Jerusalem was destined for destruction, and the holy presence of God that once filled it, now filled the hearts and spirits of people everywhere that had received God's grace.

By the end of the NT period, the letters to the churches were filled with exhortations to be true to sound doctrine, and to recognize the marks of false prophets, false teachers, false leaders, etc. Even when Jesus commissioned John to send letters to the church at Smyrna and Philadelphia, He warned the church about people claiming to be Jews, but they were really from the synagogue of satan! *(Rev. 2:9; 3:9)*

When Paul writes his second letter to the Thessalonians, it's to correct a misunderstanding that has spread concerning the Lord's return. Evidently, somebody had followed after Paul's original ministry in the city and taught that the day of the Lord had already come. *(II Thess. 2:1–2)*

Paul says it cannot come until certain things occur, which include rebellion, lawlessness, opposition to godly things, and all kinds of fake worship and phony miracles in an effort to appear godly. Paul indicates in the context that whatever this is, or whoever this is, it will be permitted to show its true colors over a period of time until Christ returns. *(II Thess. 2:3–10)*

The attack against godliness is best summed up in this passage:

> *"He will oppose and exalt himself over everything that is called God or is worshiped, so that he sets himself up in God's temple, proclaiming himself to be God."*
> *II Thess. 2:4*

This is a heavy word with a serious tone and a clear warning. But a key to understanding it lies in remembering what temple Paul was always concerned about. It's the spiritual temple—the church, the mystical body of Christ. Paul's concern was never that a personal antichrist was going to sit in another literal temple in Jerusalem. His concern was that the spirit of the antichrist would seek to infiltrate, (work its way into), the church, the spiritual temple!

Too many people today ***overestimate*** the future of an antichrist figure, and ***underestimate*** the spirit of the antichrist already at work.

And that spirit has been working for a long time. Paul points out, *"the secret power of lawlessness is already at work ..." II Thess. 2:7*

John echoes Paul's words, *"... This is the spirit of the anti-christ, which you have heard is coming and even now is already in the world." I John. 4:3*

Sounds to me like they knew the blunt statements of Jesus, and were already seeing impostors trying to sneak in by the end of the first century. Jesus had forewarned them:

> *"Watch out for false prophets. They come to you in sheep's clothing, but inwardly they are ferocious wolves. By their fruit you will recognize them." Matt.7:15–16*

The apostle Peter said it was already beginning near the end of his ministry.

> *"But there were also false prophets among the people, just as there will be false teachers among you. They will secretly introduce destructive heresies, even denying the sovereign Lord who bought them—bringing swift destruction on themselves. Many will follow their shameful ways and will bring the way of truth into disrepute. In their greed these teachers will exploit you with stories they have made up." II Pet. 2:1–3*

## WHO'S BEEN SITTING IN THE TEMPLE ?

Paul had good reason to be concerned about the true temple, the church, because the Spirit of God had already revealed to him some of the attacks the church would face during its history. Does this sound familiar?

> *"The Spirit clearly says that in later times some will abandon the faith and follow deceiving spirits and things taught by demons. Such teachings come through hypocritical liars, whose consciences have been seared as with a hot iron. They forbid people to marry and order them to abstain from certain foods, which God created to be received with thanksgiving by those who believe and know the truth." I Tim. 4:1–3*

> *"But mark this: There will be terrible times in the last days. People will be lovers of themselves, lovers of money, boastful, proud, abusive, disobedient to their parents, ungrateful, unholy, without love, unforgiving, slanderous, without self-control, not lovers of good, treacherous, rash, conceited, lovers of pleasure rather than lovers of God—having a form of godliness but denying its power. Have nothing to do with them." II Tim. 3:1–5*

When did Paul say these things would happen? In the last days.

And when are the last days? Not just the days we live in. Not just the last seven years before Christ returns. It's the entire church period, from the day of Pentecost until the return of Christ. So, currently that's over 2K years! That's how long the spirit of the antichrist has been trying to sit in the temple.

Neither Paul, or Peter tried to place a time stamp on when these things would happen. It was just clearly revealed to them that they would take place sometime during the church's history, and before Christ returns. Those that try to confine these attacks to some unknown future seven year period of time are sadly mistaken, and overlooking the very obvious things that have already taken place.

These passages, and others, show that the enemy's attack would be in the church, against the true church, and forms the picture of a fake, phony, religious system that appears to be godly, but in reality is opposed to the truth. God help all of us to never become that!

Unfortunately, just a light reading of the history of the church reveals a slow departure from the fullness of the truth, and a growing foothold by the antichrist spirit that becomes a major stronghold facing the leadership of the true church many years later. Once this thing got seated in the temple it became a many headed beast fighting to stay in power.

I hear the apostle Paul's words in his concern for the church at Corinth:

> *"I am jealous for you with a godly jealousy. I promised you to one husband, to Christ, so that I might present you as a pure virgin to him. But I am afraid that just as Eve was deceived by the serpent's cunning, your minds may somehow be led astray from your sincere and pure devotion to Christ. For if someone comes to you and preaches a Jesus other than the Jesus we preached, or if*

*you receive a different spirit from the one you received, or a different gospel from the one you accepted, you put up with it easily enough." II Cor. 11:2–4*

When the Bible became limited to the Latin language it brought people into a dark age spiritually. People no longer knew what Christ had purchased for them, or the marriage offer that he extended. The church no longer recognized the true position that the true husband, Christ, had given her. Instead, she was willing to be joined to a different Jesus—a fake husband who was bent on treating her with contempt, and creating a maze of religious abuse that milked her of all she was worth. Feeling nothing but shame and never being good enough, the shackles of low esteem gave her no vision for getting out, or able to stand with a sense of righteousness.

When the spirit of the antichrist got seated in the church, the good part of religion got commercialized and turned into a money making racket that opposed the truth, and took advantage of people by offering them a religious system that appeared spiritual, but was based on lies. It was the very opposite of the grace that God offered all mankind through the true husband, the Lord Jesus Christ.

## WHEN DID THIS TAKE PLACE ?

I'd like to suggest the time period of around 380 A.D. as the most obvious date when the spirit of the antichrist started getting seated in the temple. When the government of Rome stopped outrightly persecuting Christianity, a more secure seat was found for the spirit of the antichrist to operate through the government of Rome, and then other nations. Through this, its tentacles were latched on more securely.

Since then, it has tried to maintain control of the saints and kill the voice of the true church. At the very least, it has tried to intimidate and manipulate the true church by offering it a religious system that has a form of godliness, but denies the true saving power of Christ. What appeared to be a friend of the church actually became it's foe. There is much to learn about this and the varied nuances of this spirit are seen around the world to this day.

Before we go on, I'd like to point out that Paul is not the only apostle to be forewarned about the attack against the church by the antichrist spirit. This insight and the mystery of it was shown to the apostle John when he was commissioned to write the book of Revelation in the late first century.

*"Come, I will show you the punishment of the great prostitute who sits by many waters. With her the kings of the earth committed adultery, and the inhabitants of the earth were intoxicated with the wine of her adulteries.*

*Then the angel carried me away in the Spirit into a wilderness. There I saw a woman sitting on a scarlet beast that was covered with blasphemous names and had seven heads and ten horns. The woman was dressed in purple and scarlet, and was glittering with gold, precious stones and pearls. She held a golden cup in her hand, filled with abominable things and the filth of her adulteries."*

*"The name written on her forehead was a mystery: Babylon the great, the mother of prostitutes and the abominations of the earth. I saw that the woman was drunk with the blood of God's holy people, the blood of those who bore testimony of Jesus.*

*When I saw her, I was greatly astonished." Rev. 17:2–6*

Here lies the blatant and unvarnished truth—this "woman" is responsible for the death of the Lord's saints and the greatest persecutor of God's people! It's not a mistress on the side playing second fiddle, or an adulteress who comes and goes. No, far worse—she's a whore who plans on stripping her victim of the true wealth they could have in Christ, and paving the road to hell with nothing but good intentions and religious works done without Christ!

John is quite stunned to see that the spirit that influenced past kingdoms will rise again as the woman of false religion sits upon national governing bodies. The strength of this merger will be permitted to challenge the authority of the true church until Christ returns. The true church shares in the triumph of Christ, and with him, *"they will be his called, chosen, and faithful followers." (Rev. 17:14)*

The book of Revelation shows us that behind all this deception lies the great deceiver—*"that ancient serpent called the devil, or Satan, who leads the whole world astray." Rev.12:9* But that doesn't have to be your story! Your life could be described by *Rev. 12:11:*

*"They triumphed over him by the blood of the Lamb and by the word of their testimony; they did not love their lives so much as to shrink from death."*

By the end of Revelation 17, the prostitute morphs into a great city which entices millions of people and represents an alluring distraction that is destined for destruction. It's a picture of what men will try to build—a city that makes a name for itself, just like ancient Babel. It's attractive and deceiving enough that God has to command his people to come out of it before he brings it to its deserved judgment.

*"Then I heard another voice from heaven say: 'Come out of her my people,' so that you will not share in her sins, so that you will not receive any of her plagues; for her sins are piled up to heaven, and God has remembered her crimes." Rev. 18:4–5*

*"Rejoice over her, you heavens! Rejoice, you people of God! Rejoice, apostles and prophets! For God has judged her with the judgment she imposed on you." Rev.18:20*

## AFTER THE EARLY CHURCH—THE FIRST THOUSAND YEARS

It can be hard to interpret some of the images and prophetic pictures that are seen in books like Revelation and Daniel, but there's nothing like history to see how all of this unfolds. Daniel interpreted a vision of four kingdoms that would arise one after the other, each one replacing the previous one. But Daniel really had no way of knowing how, or when, the kingdoms would develop or come to pass. We know, because we live on this side of the vision and know how it came to pass in history.

With that in mind, consider how everything we've noted seems to have played out up to this point in the history of the church, and in light of the revelations given to Paul and John.

*By the year 380 A.D., Christianity was granted legal status and became the official religion of the Roman Empire. Constantine supported Christianity by exempting the Christian clergy from certain obligations and by declaring Sunday to be a public holiday because it was the day of the week on which Jesus was raised from the dead. During his reign, Constantine generously endowed Christian shrines, both in Rome and in the Holy Land.* Note 1

*When Rome fell as a political power, the Roman church became the dominant institution in Europe, and the bishop of Rome became the leader of the church, based on the claim that Peter, "the chief of the apostles," passed on his authority as Christ's representatives on earth to subsequent bishops of Rome. Leo the Great (440–461) was the first to argue for the primacy of the bishop of Rome over other bishops. And then Gregory the Great (590–604) was the first to assert that the bishop of Rome was the supreme pontificate of both the Western and Eastern churches. It was during this period that the church began calling the bishop of Rome the pope, from the Latin papa, meaning "father."* Note 2

Well, you can see right away that the Roman church took advantage of their new found favor and began to exploit it by exercising titles and positions that didn't belong to them. It was a clear departure from Christ's words in *Matt. 23:5–9*, and it granted an increasing control over the people who were willing to accept this.

*It was during this time, the 600's, that a new force emerged on the world scene when the "prophet" Muhammad launched a new religion, Islam, the Arabic word meaning, "surrender" or "submission" to the will of Allah. Islam used soldiers as missionaries and quickly spread across Northern Africa and into Europe in the 700's. By the 1400's, it controlled large parts of Eastern Europe and Asia Minor.* [Note 3]

My point in bringing this out is to show that the many false religions in the world may not be "seated in the temple", but they clearly manifest the spirit of the antichrist. They are opposed to Christ, and against Christ, and upon examination they show that "all religions are not equal," and they don't end up at the same destination!

It is fascinating to hear about modern Muslims seeing visions of Christ in their dreams, and recognizing that he is more than a prophet—he is the truth and the path to eternal life. God knows where the hungry heart is, and he's willing to meet them where they are.

## THE REFORMERS SAW IT COME TO PASS

*As the centuries passed, the Christian Church developed two "centers": the Western Church was headquartered in Rome, the Eastern Church in Constantinople. (Present day Istanbul)*

*The Western and Eastern churches were separated by three*

*things: distance, language, and authorities. Although their differences were enough to separate from one another by about 1054 A.D., they function very much the same in many respects.* Note 4

By the time of the Reformers,(approx.1300's), the institutionalized church looked nothing like the church that started in the book of Acts. It's filled with heresies, some of them even damnable, and for all of its pomp and extravagance, it reeks of dead works and the doctrine of demons that Paul warned about. *(I Tim. 4:1)*

It may come as a surprise that the first major reformers, John Hus and John Wycliffe were members of the Catholic Church and tried to bring reform from within the present religious system, rather than outside of it. The same was true with Martin Luther, a Catholic priest who became offended by the lies of the Catholic Church and finally decided to stand against its teaching.

*(By the way, I'm not against the Catholic people. I'm against the religious system that blinds people to the absolute truth found alone in Christ. Many Protestant churches went on to commit the same crimes as the Catholic Church, and likewise departed from the genuine faith. God help us all)*

As early leaders during the reformation period, these men suffered serious personal loss along with many others at the hand of the antichrist spirit that had "seated itself in the temple." Hus was killed by the institutional church, Wycliffe was threatened with excommunication, and forty-four years after his death, Wycliffe was declared a heretic and his body was exhumed and burned with his ashes thrown into a nearby river. Luther's life was threatened so often that he went into hiding for a long time. Hundreds of others lost their lives rather than cave in to the heretical teachings of the institutional church in that time.

To leave the Catholic Church on that day was to be called a "Protestant" which literally meant a "Pro-test-ant", against the Catholic Church and the system of religion and salvation it offered. The time of the reformation happened so long ago that most modern believers have no idea what the division was based on, or why the arguments got so heated. In the eyes of the reformers, the Catholic church and its leadership were the antichrist that Paul and John warned about, and they had every reason to believe that in their day.

## THE SPIRIT OF THE ANTICHRIST VS. THE HOLY SPIRIT OF CHRIST

In my own words, I list the following major differences between the institutionalized church the reformers faced in their day, which I call the fake church of the antichrist; and what are some of the notable marks of the true church that shows the true Spirit of Christ.

1. The pope has absolute authority on all matters of faith and conduct.

   *Response:* This is an arrogant statement and could apply to any denominational leader for that matter. All ministers and leaders only find their authority in the context of Scripture—they have no authority to speak beyond that. Even the term, "being led by the Spirit", requires a sufficient inspiration by the Holy Spirit's authority and in light of his scriptural leadings, whether others see it or not. Nobody knows the complete and entire will of God for anybody's life.

*"and how from infancy you have known the Holy Scriptures, which are able to make you wise for salvation through faith in Christ Jesus. All Scripture is God-breathed and is useful for teaching, rebuking, correcting and training in righteousness, so that the servant of God may be equipped for every good work." II Tim. 3:15–17*

2. The traditions of the church carry the same authority as Scripture.

   *Response:* It's hard to ignore the words of Jesus when he pointed out the same blindness, and stubbornness to the religious leaders in his day.

   *"Why do your disciples break the tradition of the elders? They don't wash their hands before they eat!" Jesus replied, "And why do you break the command of God for the sake of your tradition? For God said, 'Honor your father and mother and anyone who curses their father or their mother is to be put to death.' But you say that if anyone declares what might have been used to help their father or mother is 'devoted to God,' they are not to honor their father or mother with it. Thus you nullify the word of God for the sake of your tradition. "Matt. 15:2–7*

Even some past traditions that were rooted in the past spiritual community are only viewed as a shadow of the past. The reality is found in Christ. *(Col. 2:16–17)*

3. It is not faith alone, but participation in the sacraments of the Catholic Church that provides the only way to salvation.

   *Response: "But when the kindness and love of God our Savior appeared, he saved us, not because of righteous things we had done, but because of his mercy. He saved us through the washing of rebirth and renewal by the Holy Spirit, whom he poured out on us generously through Jesus Christ our Savior, so that, having been justified by his grace, we might become heirs having the hope of eternal life." Titus 3:5–7*

4. Each person is unworthy on their own. They must come through the priesthood of The Catholic Church, who alone are worthy to administer the sacraments to each person.

   *Response:* Paul stated emphatically that there is *"one mediator between God and mankind, the man Christ Jesus". (I Tim. 2:4)*

   Referring to the limitations of a human priesthood, the writer of Hebrews said: *"Now there have been many of those priests, since death prevented them from continuing in office; but because Jesus lives forever, he has a permanent priesthood. Therefore he is able to save completely those who come to God through him, because he always lives to intercede for them. (Hebs. 7:23–25)*

*"Therefore, since we have a great high priest who has ascended into heaven, Jesus the Son of God, let us hold firmly to the faith we profess." (Hebs. 4:14)*

5. Mary is the co-redeemer with Christ. She was born immaculate and without sin. She has always been a virgin

   *Response:* Clearly a tradition that developed in the church somewhere along the line. Scripture shows she was chosen among women, not above other women. She rejoiced in God her Savior because she needed one. Scripture is very clear that after her miracle birth and delivery, she and Joseph came together as married couples do, and brought forth other children after the virgin birth of Christ. Concerning Joseph, it says: *"But he did not consummate the marriage until she gave birth to a son. And they gave him the name Jesus." Matt.1:25* When Jesus came to his hometown, the people of Nazareth recognized his brothers and sisters when they asked: *"Isn't this the carpenter? Isn't this Mary's son and the brother of James, Joseph, Judas, and Simon? Aren't his sisters with us? And they took offense at him." (Mark 6:3)*

Additionally, it's worth noting that Mary is not mentioned one time after Acts chapter 1. None of the titles ever ascribed to Christ, or any of the glory due to him in heaven is shared with Mary at any time, not now, or in the future.

6. The priests are the only ones ordained and called for ministry.

   *Response:* Paul mentioned to the entire congregation at Corinth that they had been given the ministry of reconciliation and God would now use them as ambassadors. *(II Cor. 5:18–19)* The day of Pentecost recognized this new priesthood by God calling all of his sons and daughters to carry the prophetic spirit by proclaiming the testimony of Jesus. *(Acts 2:17–18)* Jesus promised that supernatural signs could potentially follow all of his people, not merely the first apostles or only church leaders. *(Mark 16:15–20)*

I could go on and on with the spiritual abuses that all the reformers were standing against. Various forms of manipulation, idolatry, and greed were evident for centuries, repeatedly carried out by hypocrites, like wolves in sheep's clothing. Like so much phony religion it comes down to this kind of strategy:

> What can I hide from you to keep you in the spiritual dark?
>
> How can I make you feel worse about yourself than

you already do?

How can I make you feel guilty enough to give me some more money?

How can I make you believe that my control over you would be a good thing?

On and on it goes …

When John Wycliffe got the Bible translated into English, and no longer limited to Latin, the common man had a chance to see the light that had been there all the time. A two-edged sword was now at his hand, and with this, the reformers fought back against the wiles of the devil.

> *"In addition to all this, take up the shield of faith, with which you can extinguish all the flaming arrows of the wicked one. Take the helmet of salvation and the sword of the Spirit, which is the word of God." Ephesians 6:16–17*

After looking at these differences, it's important to remember that there are many people, attending many different kinds of churches, by many different names. Many of them don't pay much attention to many doctrinal issues, but if they are sincerely seeking God for salvation and embrace Christ as their Savior, he meets them where they are at. It's our relationship with him that saves us, not our perfect doctrinal understanding, or our denominational bias.

The finished work of Christ *alone* provides the secure foundation for our salvation and eternal life. We may add, or may not add, many things when building our spiritual house, but whether it's all reduced to nothing but the foundation, or crowned with many rewards, salvation is only found in him and to him alone belongs all the glory. *(I Cor. 3:11–15)*

## WHO ELSE HAS RELIGION BEEN SHACKING UP WITH?

You really don't have to look very hard to see the spirit of the antichrist that still seeks to,"sit in the temple." When I was a kid I could always count on getting two things every Christmas—new underwear and new socks. The wrapping paper may have changed, but each year the gift was still the same inside. Nothing has changed. The spiritual landscape is littered with religious ideas that are devoid of the Spirit of God, and just appealing enough to deceive too many people.

Religion that is state sponsored and in bed with worldly governments continues to wreck havoc upon thousands of genuine and sincere believers in Christ. We need to remember to pray for them and support them, while we fight with the truth that can set others truly free. Remember, the prostitute sits on "meaning waters", meaning nations and empires.

I see this as a picture of the many religions of the world trying to satisfy man with something other than the pure grace of God offered through Christ. Like the wrapping paper at Christmas, it may appear different from one country to another,—and from one kind of temple to another—but it's the same life-killing spirit at work trying to deceive mankind.

## THE DAY THE MUSIC DIES

In the parable of the tares and wheat, Jesus taught that both of them would grow together until the end of time. During the period up to the harvest time, there's a temptation for unbridled zeal to uproot some things that appear less than pure wheat. We can trust at harvest time that Christ alone is capable of making all things completely right, and we'll be very happy with the outcome! *(Matt. 13:36–43)*

Whenever Christ decides to return, the music will stop playing and it's game over for whoever is sitting in the chair on that day. Those who claim to be in authority will be stripped of their power, and the saints who already have Christ seated in their hearts, will alone rule and reign with Christ because they've overcome. It will be apparent at that time that Christ alone, who sits at the right hand of the Father, is the only Christ worthy to rule over all the earth, and sit in the true temple. Amen.

# 9

# THE RESURRECTION & THE RAPTURE

*THE PROMISE OF A NEW ETERNAL BODY*

## THE RESURRECTION OF CHRIST—BEDROCK OF OUR FAITH

THE RESURRECTION OF Christ is the very foundation for the Christian's faith. Without the resurrection of Christ everything else is a complete waste of our time. The apostle Paul stated emphatically that our faith is in vain, we have no hope, and we've been found preaching a lie if Christ has not been raised from the dead. *(See I Cor. 15:14–19)* If Christ was not raised from the dead when he came the first time, then there's no reason to expect his coming a second time.

The resurrection of Christ, and the evidence that supports it, should be the core reason for why you are a believer today. Not that you were raised in a Christian home, or have had a spiritual conviction or experience, or were pressured by a church or special interest group. All of that is subject to change and has its own imperfections. The resurrection of Christ stands completely on its own, and commands everyone to make a decision about it and how they will live in the light of it.

The resurrection of the dead is described as a foundational doctrine and elementary teaching for the Christian. *(Hebs.6:3)* When you have a good understanding of it, you can see how it affects the way we live and how it affects our future. And yet for all of that, there is a surprising amount of confusion and lack of clarity about it.

## THE OLD TESTAMENT GIVES THE PROMISE OF RESURRECTION

The resurrection appears as one of the earliest questions in man's heart. The ancient patriarch Job asked: *"If a man dies will he live again? All the days of my hard service I will wait for my renewal to come." Job 14:14*

The very creation that man is a steward of indicates the possibility of a resurrection. The seasonal changes indicate that things that appear dead can return to form year after year. The simple example of the caterpillar being transformed into the butterfly expresses the same truth.

Later on, Job answers his own question by boldly proclaiming: *"I know that my Redeemer lives, and that in the end he will stand upon the earth. And after my skin has been destroyed, yet in my flesh I will see God; I myself will see him with my own eyes—I and not another. How my heart yearns within me!" Job 19:25–27*

The prophet Daniel adds his own testimony in the last chapter of his book:

*"Multitudes who sleep in the dust of the earth will awake: some to everlasting life, and some to everlasting contempt." Daniel 12:2*

The truth of this seems to have been known well enough by

the time of Jesus' ministry. When Lazarus died, his sister Martha said to Jesus, *"I know he will rise again in the resurrection on the last day." John 11:24.*

## JESUS IS THE RESURRECTION AND THE LIFE

It's at this point in the story of Lazarus that Jesus personified the resurrection with himself when he said: *"I am the resurrection and the life. ..." John 11:25*. And to prove it, he raised Lazarus when he had already been dead for four days! This became an undeniable miracle that even the religious leaders opposed to Christ could not refute. *(John 12:9–10)*

Furthermore, in teaching about the truth of the resurrection, Jesus emphasized two kinds of resurrection—a spiritual one, and a natural or physical one.

***Spiritual*** – *"Very truly I tell you, a time is coming and has now come when the dead will hear the voice of the Son of God and those who hear will live." John 5:25 "... and whoever lives and believes in me will never die." John 11:26*

When Jesus used the phrase, *"has now come"*, whatever was being offered was available immediately.

In these passages the focus is on the ***spiritual*** resurrection which reminds us of the apostle Paul's letter to the Ephesians when he said, *"... God, who is rich in mercy, made us alive with Christ even when we were dead in transgressions—it is by grace you have been saved. And God raised us up with Christ and seated us with him ...". Eph. 2:4–6*

***Natural, Physical*** – *"Do not be amazed at this, for* ***a time is coming*** *when all who are* ***in their graves*** *will hear his voice and come out—those who have done what is good will rise to live, and those* *who have done what is evil will rise to be condemned." John 5:28–29*

## WHAT THE RESURRECTION OF CHRIST PROVED

Many times Jesus clearly predicted his rejection, betrayal, crucifixion, and his physical resurrection. One was promised just as much as the other. The NT apostles stated that the resurrection confirmed the prophecies God had given the nation of Israel, and that it was necessary, first of all, to prove that Jesus was the unique Son of God and the promised Messiah to come. *(See Acts 2:24–36; Ps. 16:8–11)*

Other prophets had come before and healed the sick, multiplied provisions, worked miracles, and even raised the dead. But they all died and remained that way. Christ alone had been raised.

## THE APPEARANCES OF THE RESURRECTED CHRIST

The appearances of the risen Christ took place over many days and he was seen by many different people, even up to 500 hundred people at once. Paul mentions six appearances in *I Corinthians 15:5–8*, and along with the gospel accounts, there are a total of 13 different appearances mentioned in the NT record. Luke calls this, *"many convincing proofs"*, in Acts 1:3. It's not the focus of this book to examine closely the reliability of the resurrection of Christ, but I do encourage you to look closely at it. I will address the common objection that it was all a conspiracy carried out by his disciples.

Conspiracies by their very nature cannot survive over long periods of time by large groups. Somebody will cough up the secret and expose the lies. In the natural world, the twelve apostles and the Lord's natural family had absolutely nothing to gain from spreading a conspiracy, and everything to lose, including their lives. No amount of fame, money, or control would have been worth going through what they did.

Church history as always confirmed all of them died a martyr's death, or were imprisoned for their faith. Many people will die for what they believe to be the truth, but nobody would die for what they *know* is a lie!

## WHAT KIND OF BODY DID THE RESURRECTED CHRIST HAVE?

This is actually very important to us, because the fact that Christ has been raised from the dead, his resurrection becomes the pledge for us, and whatever distinctive features his resurrected body has, these become a pattern of what we can expect in the future for ourselves. As Paul told the church at Corinth:

> *"But Christ has indeed been raised from the dead, the first fruits of those who have fallen asleep. For since death came through a man, the resurrection of the dead comes also through a man. For as in Adam all die, so in Christ all will be made alive." I Cor. 15:20–22*

**The nature of the resurrected body when Christ appeared:** His body was capable of being recognized and had the same essential form that all human bodies have—the same as before. Yes, it's true that initially they didn't recognize him, but that's because they didn't expect him, or anyone, to come back from the kind of death he suffered. Anybody that has lost a close loved one un-expectantly, knows that the grief of death is very paralyzing. But the disciples didn't stay that way, they became convinced quickly.

> His body was capable of eating real physical food and being tangible enough to touch and feel—*Luke 24:37–40*
>
> His body was capable of passing through locked doors—*John 20:19*
>
> His body will uniquely maintain the scars of crucifixion—*John 20:25–26*
>
> The mechanics of his body, and how it functioned, were the same as before, although now he could ascend—*John 20:6–14; Acts 1:9–10*

## THE STATE OF THE DEAD IN CHRIST—I THESS. 4:13–17

It's important to understand the terms Paul uses to convey his message. He calls ***one group, "the dead in Christ"***, or those who have fallen *"asleep in him"*. We know that Paul is referring to physical death, because a believer is ***never*** described *spiritually* as "dead in Christ"—that's impossible. As I mentioned previously, the believer is always described *spiritually* as being alive in Christ. *(Eph. 2:5–6)*

**The word *"asleep"* is used for two different reasons:** When someone is asleep it looks like they have actually died in the sense that their eyes are closed, they're not moving, and most of their bodily functions are suspended for the moment; the same as when people actually do die. You might have said this very type phrase—*"I slept so hard I was dead to the world."*

The other reason *"asleep"* is used, is to show us that death doesn't mean you cease to exist and no longer function at all; but rather that you've entered into a temporary state of being, a transition, from which you'll return shortly. Like sleeping, you might be unconscious to your surroundings and what is taking place, but at the same time you're not completely removed without the hope of ever returning. Again, you might have said after sleeping for 10 hours, *"All this happened while I was asleep?!"*

Asleep is the term that Jesus used in referring to the death of Lazarus. *(See John 11:11–14)*

God's plan is that, *"whether we are awake or asleep, we may live together with him." I Thess. 5:10.* This echoes the statement Jesus made at the last supper in *John 14:2–6, "In my Father's house are many rooms, if it were not so, I would have told you. I am going to prepare a place for you. And if I go and prepare a place for you, I will come back and take you to be with me that you may also be where I am."*

Well, that's certainly not a graveyard. Not only does Jesus want you to be *where* he is, but *how* he is also, and he's very much alive! Some people get the mistaken idea that people enter some kind of soul sleep at death where they know nothing and experience nothing. This is not what Jesus taught about both the righteous and the unrighteous. In the parable about the rich man and Lazarus, the sensory faculties of both of them were very much alive and functioning. *(See Luke 16:19–31)* They will function in us as well.

## THE DESIRE OF THE RIGHTEOUS

In writing to the church at Thessalonica, Paul called this preferred place, "being at home with the Lord."

> *"Therefore we are always confident and know that as long as we are at home in the body we are away from the Lord. We live by faith and not by sight. We are confident, I say, and would prefer to be away from the body and at home with the Lord. So we make it our goal to please him, whether we are at home in the body or away from it."*
> *II Cor. 5:8–9*

If being at *"home with the Lord"* is nothing more than soul sleep or inactivity, then Paul would not have desired this, and he certainly wouldn't recommend it to us either.

This raises another question that frequently comes up when this thought is explored.

What do the righteous or those *"dead in Christ"* spend all their time doing if they're so alive? I would say essentially the same kind of things we should be doing here, *"in the body"*, which is pleasing the Lord. *(II Cor. 5:9)* I think it would include actively growing, changing, and serving, but certainly not sitting around continually. Of course it includes reunions with loved ones, worshipping our Creator, and being blown away with the incredible glories of heaven, but it's a place of godly service and sanctified activity as well.

The main reason we get tired of doing a lot of those things here is because we are burdened too much in this "earthly tent"

*(II Cor. 5:4)*. We spend far too much time carrying anxiety and trying to make others happy instead of the Lord. Like it's been said, when we're young, we wonder what others think of us, and when we're old, we realize they were never thinking about us anyway!

When we're in heaven our motives are purified, and our actions are not about earning our salvation, or trying to prove anything to anybody else. We grow, love, and serve because we realize how much God loves us *already*, and that desire leads us to please him. *(I John 4:10,19)* It's not a "have to" salvation we are living, it's a "want to", and "get to" kind of salvation.

Here's a few questions to ponder:

> What about all the spiritual growth that believers could have had here and never really cared about?
>
> What about all the opportunities people passed up to be involved in serving others, and using their abilities to help others?
>
> What about all the people who make heaven their home late in life and know almost nothing of the eternal plan of God, or the benefits paid for by Christ in his redemption for them?

Again, it's not about *working for* my salvation, it's about *walking out* the salvation he *already* provided at the cross. *(Phil. 2:12–13)* It is God's will that we grow, and that, *"in all things we grow up into him that is the Head, that is, Christ." (Eph. 4:15)* But in all things our spiritual growth is based on the generous grace that God offers us eternally through Christ.

**The second group Paul** mentions to the Thessalonians are

those described as, *"still alive and left till the coming of the Lord". I Thess. 4:15,17.* Whoever is destined to be in this special group at God's determined time, they will have a supernatural experience that very few of the faithful have previously had. This will take place immediately following the resurrection of the dead in Christ. Paul says, *"… we who are still alive and are left will be caught up together with them in the clouds to meet the Lord in the air." I Thess. 4:17*

Paul uses the term, *"caught up"*, and this expression is rarely used in the Bible. Modern readers more commonly use the word, "rapture" to mean the same thing.

## WHAT IS THE RAPTURE?

Some people like to get cute and point out that the word rapture is not even found in the Bible. The word for the divine Godhead, Trinity, is not found in the Bible either, but the truth and concept of it is found from Genesis to Revelation. So, that's not a strong talking point. The English word, rapture, comes from a Latin expression which means to be "caught up." That experience actually has a notable history in the Bible and following are some examples you may, or may not know about.

*"By faith Enoch* ***was taken*** *from this life, so that* ***he did not experience death;*** *he could not be found, because God had* ***taken him away.*** *For before he was taken, he was commended as one who pleased God." Hebs. 11:5*

> *"As they were walking along and talking together, suddenly a chariot of fire and horses of fire appeared and separated*

> *the two of them, and **Elijah went up to heaven** in a whirlwind. Elisha saw this and cried out, "My father! My father! The chariots and horsemen of Israel!" And Elisha saw him no more. …" II Kings 2:11–12*

Evidently, the company of prophets in training believed this could happen, or possibly may have happened previously, for they said to Elisha:"… *we your servants have fifty able men. Let them go and look for your master. Perhaps the Spirit of the Lord has **picked him up** and set him down on some mountain or valley." II Kings 2:16.* See also *I Kings 18:12*

> *"Then both Philip and the eunuch went down into the water and Philip baptized him. When they came up out of the water, the Spirit of the Lord **suddenly took Philip away**, and the eunuch did not see him again, but went on his way rejoicing. Philip however, appeared at Azotus and traveled about, preaching the gospel in all the towns until he reached Caesarea." Acts 8:38–40*

I think the apostle Paul's recounting of his experience qualifies as a *"caught up"* experience as well: *"I know a man in Christ who fourteen years ago was **caught up** to the third heaven. Whether it was in the body or out of the body—God knows. And I know that this man—whether in the body or apart from the body I do not know, but God knows—was **caught up** to paradise." II Cor. 12:2–4*

Finally we need to include the apostle John when he was commissioned to write the book of Revelation. It's possible he could have had all the visions while stuck in the rocky prison of Patmos, but the view would have been much more majestic from a truly heavenly viewpoint. Although the specific phrase "caught up" is not used, the language of the verse carries the same meaning.

> *"After this I looked, and there before me was a door standing open in heaven. And the voice I had first heard speaking to me like a trumpet said, "**Come up here**, and I will show you what must take place after this." **At once I was in the Spirit,** and there before me was a throne in heaven with someone sitting on it." Rev. 4:1–2*

These examples from the Bible rarely took place and it's doubtful it had anything to do with the depth of spirituality each of these men possessed. I have heard of a couple other instances of this occurring since the book of Acts, but I cannot verify that confidently.

Each of these cases show us *what* God is capable of doing, but none of them are a guarantee of what he will do for any one individual, and certainly not *when* he might do it. The only promise that we can definitely count on is that sometime in the future this event, the rapture, will take place as part of the resurrection of the dead. The catching up of the living saints is actually secondary to the resurrection of the dead, which clearly takes place ***first***.

> *"According to the Lord's own word, we tell you that we who are still alive, who are left till the coming of the Lord, will certainly **not precede those who have***

> ***fallen asleep.*** *For the Lord himself will come down from heaven, with a loud command, with the voice of the archangel, and with the trumpet call of God, and* ***the dead in Christ will rise first. After that, we who are still alive*** *and are left will be caught up together with them ..." (I Thess. 4:15–17)*

There can be no argument, or misinterpretation, with regard to that. So in painful simplicity let me point out:

> The rapture does not take place before the resurrection.
>
> The rapture does not take place instead of the resurrection
>
> The rapture does not take place separately from the resurrection, (like seven years ahead of it.)
>
> There is no rapture without the resurrection first. The resurrection is the whole reason for the rapture!

### WHAT IS THE PURPOSE OF THE RAPTURE ?

The modern church in America has a very misplaced focus on the purpose for the rapture, and here is where they veer off onto a pathway that is not supported anywhere in the context of Scripture.

The purpose of the rapture is ***not a defensive maneuver*** to escape tribulation. It's a ***transformational change*** to bring you into the new eternal body that Christ promised you.

Have you ever considered what Jesus prayed for all of us before he went to the cross?

*"My prayer is* ***not that you take them out of the world*** *but that you protect them from the evil one." John 17:15.*

This is what Jesus is praying, which seems very different from a lot of the prayers and hopes of other people. I wonder whose prayer will get answered?!

As I'll bring out later, the true church has always suffered persecution. Yes, there are times in history when it's been a lot worse, but there are many countries today where it's very possible, even probable, that you may lose your life as an outspoken Christian. So, it's ignorance gone to seed to think that an entire army of people will be snatched away and not have to face the opposition that millions of others had to.

**By the way, have you ever thought about this:**

If you're praying for a big spiritual harvest, who do you think will be commissioned to gather it in? People need spiritual mentors, and mothers and fathers in the faith when they enter the kingdom. Who do you think God will direct to care for them?

If not you, then who?

If not here and now, then where and when?

## WHY DO THE RIGHTEOUS NEED A NEW BODY?

You will need a new body to live on the new earth, which will have experienced a complete renewal. The apostle Peter expressed it this way:

*"You ought to live holy and godly lives as you look forward*

*to the day of God and speed its coming. That day will bring about the destruction of the heavens by fire, and the elements will melt in the heat. But in keeping with his promise we are looking forward to a new heaven and a new earth, the home of righteousness. "II Pet. 3:11–13*

The new earth is not only the home of righteousness; it's the *home* of the righteous.

Up until that time you won't need a new kind of body, but as soon as the earth is renewed, it'll require you to have a new body that can assimilate and identify with a new earth.

You'll need a new body fitted for a new earth. Your old body cannot inherit the fullness of God's kingdom. Paul said, *"I declare to you, brothers, that flesh and blood cannot inherit the kingdom of God, nor does the perishable inherit the imperishable" I Cor. 15:50*

Think of it this way—your old body is not "wired" for the power of the new earth. Everything you've had up till now is only a foretaste, or a down payment, of the power of that glory—the glory of a superior, eternal body, that will never know death. **Notice the statements that Paul used to describe this new body that you'll have:**

Raised imperishable

Raised in glory

Raised in power

Raised a spiritual body

Raised to bear the likeness of the heavenly man (Jesus)
*I Cor. 15:42–49*

Notice the words, weak, dead and buried are not included.

The apostle John gives us the insight he received when he was instructed to write the book of Revelation and send it to the churches. This helps us understand life on the new earth.

> *"Then I saw a new heaven and **a new earth,** for the first heaven and **the first earth had passed away,** and there was no longer any sea. I saw the Holy City, the new Jerusalem **coming down out of heaven** from God, prepared as a bride beautifully dressed for her husband.*
>
> *And I heard a loud voice from the throne saying, **Now the dwelling of God is with men,** and he will live with them. They will be his people, and God himself will be with them and be their God. He will wipe every tear from their eyes. There will be no more death or mourning or crying or pain, for **the old order of things has passed away."** Rev. 21:1–4*

This is ***the real reason*** the resurrection and the rapture takes place. ***It's not to take you to heaven. It's about bringing heaven to you!*** Now I can hear some people moaning in the background bummed because you thought you'd spend eternity up in heaven, and staying on the earth was not on your "bucket list".

But imagine, if you will, how beautiful life on earth would be if all the earthly evils were gone and only the absolute beauty of God's grace and love permeated the entire planet. Your body would only experience strength, vitality, and youthful beauty—no sickness, disease, imperfections, or the disabilities of old age. And then on top of that, all your friends and family members who have passed away, are now united together with you in all of their eternal youthfulness as well. That's a nice looking group of people!

Of course, before that, and beyond all this, is being in the direct presence of your Savior, Jesus, who generously gave himself for you, and has returned as your victorious king!

I think this is what many people call "heaven".

Paul expressed it this way to the Corinthian Christians:

> *"However, as it is written: No eye has seen, no ear has heard, no mind has conceived what God has prepared for those who love him—but God has revealed it to us by his Spirit." I Cor. 2:9–10*

God has already shown us enough of the future that we can trust him completely and prepare accordingly.

## WHEN DOES THE RESURRECTION AND RAPTURE TAKE PLACE?

In writing to the Thessalonians, Paul clearly established *the order of the resurrection* with the dead in Christ rising *first*, and then followed by the living saints. *(I Thess. 4:15–17)* As we would expect, when he writes the letter to the Corinthians he places the sequence of events in the same exact order as before.

> *"Listen, I tell you a mystery: We will not all sleep, but we will all be changed—in a flash, in the twinkling of an eye, at the last trumpet. For the trumpet will sound, and the*

*dead will be raised imperishable, and we will be changed. For the perishable must clothe itself with imperishable, and the mortal with immortality." I Cor. 15:51–53.*

The dead in Christ will be changed *first*, followed by the living saints who have not experienced death yet. It all seems like a mystery now, because it's never been experienced by any group of people, but if you believe and know that God created the present heavens and the earth, then obviously a new kind of body is short work for him.

The words of Christ, and the apostle Paul, present the easiest order to follow with regard to the resurrection and the rapture. Nothing stated in the book of Revelation will contradict that. The message of Revelation is presented in a unique language style all of its own, so the gospels and epistles are easier to follow for most people.

Before really getting in-depth about the resurrection body for believers, the apostle Paul states a simple order of end time events to the Corinthians.

*"For as in Adam all die, so in Christ all will be made alive. But each in his own turn: Christ, the first fruits, then when He comes, those who belong to him." I Cor. 15:22–23*

Who are those who belong to him? The dead in Christ, and those saints who are still alive. *"Then the end will come, …" (I Cor. 15:24).* This means the second coming of Christ and all the events that accompany it. Here, Paul clearly connects the resurrection with the end of all things.

> *"Then the end will come, when he hands over the kingdom to God the Father after he has destroyed all dominion, authority and power. For he must reign until he has put all his enemies under his feet. The last enemy to be destroyed is death." I Cor. 15:24–26*

Paul went on to say that when the resurrection happens, "***... then*** *the saying that is written will come true: "Death has been swallowed up in victory." Where, o death is your victory? Where, o death is your sting?" I Cor. 15:54–55*

Until the resurrection takes place we still feel the "sting" of death, but that's all it really is, because we continue to live in the presence of God with the living hope of the resurrection at the proper time.

The resurrection destroys the power of death, and if death is the last enemy to be destroyed, then clearly the resurrection is connected with the end of all things, and the arrival of the new heavens and new earth. Paul states the resurrection and this supernatural change will take place at, "... *the last trumpet. For the trumpet will sound and the dead will be raised imperishable and we will be changed." I Cor. 15:52*

## WHEN ARE THE ELECT ARE GATHERED?

The words of Paul fall right into line with the teachings of Jesus. Jesus repeatedly taught that the resurrection would happen on the last day, at the last trumpet, at his second coming. Consider the following:

> *"And this is the will of him who sent me, that I shall lose none of all that he has given me, but will* ***raise them up at the last day.*** *For my Father's will is that everyone who looks to the Son and believes in him shall have eternal life, and I will* ***raise him up at the last day.*** *" John 6:39–40*

> *"No one can come to me unless the Father who sent me draws him, and I will* ***raise him up at the last day."*** *John 6:44*

> *"Whoever eats my flesh and drinks my blood has eternal life, and I will* ***raise him up at the last day."*** *John 6:54*

I think he's trying to tell us something!

Prior to this teaching, Jesus testified that the call for resurrection would go out to everyone.

> *"Do not be amazed at this, for a time is coming when* ***all who are in their graves*** *will hear his voice and come out— those who have done good will rise to live, and those who have done evil will rise to be condemned." John 5:28–29*

When the disciples asked Jesus about the end of the age, he addressed many things that I've already mentioned, but regarding the day of his return He said it would follow after the distress of what he previously indicated. *(Matt. 24:29)* He went on to say:

> *"At that time the sign of the Son of Man will appear in the sky, and all the nations of the earth will mourn. They will see the Son of Man coming on the clouds of the sky, with power and great glory. And he will send his angels with a* ***loud trumpet call****, and they will* ***gather his elect*** *from the four winds, from one end of the heavens to the other." Matt. 24:30–31*

Here's the resurrection with the rapture. This is expressed as a worldwide event, not a localized gathering of only Jews, (the former "elect") or 144,000—a number that some groups try to apply literally. All of God's elect will be raised up and experience the power of his resurrection, resulting in a new, eternal physical body—one prepared for the new earth.

## WHO IS ACTUALLY TAKEN AWAY WHEN CHRIST RETURNS?

In the parables of the kingdom recorded in Matthew 13, Jesus gives us a very simple set of details that have far ranging effects when he returns to earth. It's the parable of the weeds in the field and its entirety is found in **Matt. 13:37–43**

> *"As the weeds are pulled up and burned in the fire, so it will be at the end of the age. The Son of Man will send out his angels, and they will weed out of his kingdom everything that causes sin and all who do evil. They will throw them into the fiery furnace, where there will be weeping and gnashing of teeth. Then the righteous will*

> *shine like the sun in the kingdom of their Father. He who has ears, let him hear." Matt. 13:40–43*

In every single passage that Jesus taught about his second coming, it is *always* the evildoer who is *taken away*, and it is *always* the righteous who *remain* and live on the new earth. Does this sound familiar? *"Blessed are the meek, for they will inherit the earth." Matt. 5:5*

Jesus compared his return and coming to the days of Noah before the flood. He said the people in Noah's time:

> *"knew nothing about what would happen until the flood came and* ***took them all away****. That is how it will be at the coming of the Son of Man. Two men will be in the field:* ***one will be taken*** *and the other left. Two women will be grinding with a hand mill;* ***one will be taken*** *and the other left." Matt. 24:39–41*

In each of these illustrations, the one who is taken away went into judgment, and the one who is righteous and prepared remains, and is "left behind"!

## WHO'S HOUSE IS BROKEN INTO BY THE THIEF?

It's always the one who is unprepared, and shows it by living a life of carelessness and unbelief. The believer *totally expects* the return of his Lord, and lives accordingly. Believers will not know the exact day and hour, but because they know the master *will return*, his arrival will not take them by complete surprise like when a thief breaks in.

In their letters, Paul and Peter both seem to have this in mind.

> *"First of all, you must understand that in the last days scoffers will come, scoffing and following their one desires. They will say, "Where is this 'coming' he promised? But the day of the Lord will come like a thief." II Pet. 3:3–4, 10*

Well it does to the person who is living like that.

> *"But you brothers, are not in darkness so that this day should surprise you like a thief. You are all sons of the light and sons of the day. We do not belong to the night or to the darkness. So then, let us not be like others, who are asleep, but let us be alert and self-controlled." I Thess. 5:4–6*

It's the scoffer, mockers and evildoers that are taken by surprise, not the righteous. Believers fully expect the Lord's return, even if they do not know the hour or the day. As such, they prepare accordingly with lives that show it.

## THE REWARD OF THE RIGHTEOUS

When you read the 37th Psalm, it's clear that the psalmist wanted all of us to know that God is aware of the imbalances in society. As difficult as it is, we're called to place our hope in God and to know that his character includes a love that makes all things right at the end.

*"A little while, and the wicked will be no more; though you look for them, they will not be found. But the meek will inherit the land and enjoy great peace." Ps. 37:10–11*

David had such a knowledge of God's promises that he expressed his faith repeatedly in this psalm by saying six different times that the righteous will inherit the land! *Ps. 37:9, 11, 22, 27, 29, 34.*

In his day, David was probably focusing on the land of Israel under the covenant God had made with them, but the NT shows us that the kingdom Jesus brings is much larger and includes all the earth, and the meek and humble will be joint heirs with him.

God is not in debt to anybody, and if he has asked us to give something up, it's because he has something better for us in the future. I'm sure many people would echo the same question that Peter asked of Jesus, and get the same kind of answer that Jesus gave Peter.

*"Peter answered him, "We have left everything to follow you! What then will there be for us?"*

*Jesus said the them, "I tell you the truth, at the renewal of all things, when the Son of Man sits on his glorious throne, you who have followed me will also sit on twelve thrones, judging the twelve tribes of Israel,*

*And everyone who has left houses or brothers or sisters or father or mother or children or fields for my sake will receive a hundred times as much and will inherit eternal life. But many who are first will be last, and many who are last will be first. Matt. 19:27–30*

Finally, in writing to the church at Philippi, Paul wants them to be aware that this present world is growing older and decaying, however, our real citizenship is much greater.

*"But our citizenship is in heaven. And we eagerly await a Savior from there, the Lord Jesus Christ, who, by the power that enables him to bring everything under his control, will transform our lowly bodies so that they will be like his glorious body." Phil. 3:20–21*

The future looks bright, indeed!

# 10

# WHO EXPERIENCES GREAT TRIBULATION?

**THE OT HEBREW** words that describe the idea of tribulation are best translated as "distress", or "trouble". Both words draw attention to the emotional response of the person who is under pressure. The pressure may come from enemies, adverse circumstances, wrong decisions, etc. The noun and the verb both suggest circumstances that are confining and narrow. It's the idea of being stuck in a corner with no way out.

In the NT, the primary word used to define tribulation is the Greek word, *thlipsis*, which is most often translated, "distress" and "trouble". As in the OT, it conveys the idea of great emotional and spiritual stress that can be caused by external or internal pressures.

A good example of this is seen in the life of the apostle Paul when he wrote the church in *II Thess. 1:6 "God is just: He will pay back trouble to those who trouble you and give relief to you who are troubled, and to us as well."*

In warning about the destruction of Jerusalem in the first century, Jesus told his disciples that *"then there will be great distress" or tribulation (Matt. 24:21).* Furthermore, Jesus stated that his return would be, *"after the distress of those days"*, that preceded his return. *(Matt. 24:29)*

The intensity of this kind of pressure and the emotional stress it can create is seen in Paul's words to the church at Corinth:

> *"We do not want you to be uninformed, brothers, about the hardships we suffered in the province of Asia. We were under great pressure, far beyond our ability to endure, so that we despaired even of life. Indeed in our hearts we felt the sentence of death. But this happened that we might not rely on ourselves but on God, who raises the dead. He has delivered us from such a deadly peril, and he will deliver us." II Cor. 1:8–10*

When a person feels like they are moments from death and under serious pressure to compromise their faith, I would certainly define that as heavy pressure and intense distress, wouldn't you?! That's a pressure that few of us in the modern churches of the West has had to face, but we have many brothers and sisters in Christ who are already facing great tribulation and great distress where they live now.

This kind of tribulation is not limited to some kind of time frame, like a seven year period suggested by some views. It's defined by the kind of intensity that is life-threatening pressure, which refuses to compromise the faith, and is even willing to pass through the door of death, unless God delivers them.

Writing to Timothy late in his life, Paul summarizes the intense distress he was sometimes under when he says: *"persecutions and sufferings, such as happened to me at Antioch, at Iconium and at Lystra; what persecutions I endured, and out of them all the Lord delivered me!" II Tim. 3:11*

## FOREWARNED AND FOREARMED

Tribulation and distress at this level has been a consistent and opposing force since the inception of the church. There are countless statements where Jesus forewarned his followers that their message and lives would be persecuted and hated by others.

> *"If the world hates you, keep in mind that it hated me first. If you belonged to the world, it would love you as its own. … Remember the words I spoke to you: 'No servant is greater than his master.' If they persecuted me, they will persecute you also." John 15:18–20*

Jesus pointed out that people in their intense hatred and ignorance will actually think they are on the right side of things to act the way they do.

> *"All this I have told you so that you will not go astray. They will put you out of the synagogue, in fact, a time is coming when anyone who kills you will think he is offering a service to God. They will do such things because they have not known the Father or me. I have told you this, so that when the time comes you will remember that I warned you." John 16:1–4*

I'm not implying that persecution and trouble has to be at this level to qualify, but people can push persecution to such a level that they see what they do as, "good", when in reality it is "evil". *(Isaiah 5:20)*

Just the fact that you've chosen to enter the kingdom of God is not pleasing to the enemy of your soul. But the fact that you did enter proves that he doesn't have all power—only God is all mighty! Paul says the essence of it starts with our decision to live life differently than before. *"In fact, everyone who wants to live a godly life in Christ Jesus will be persecuted." II Tim. 3:12*

It doesn't happen because we did anything wrong. It happens because Jesus Christ chose us, and in their blinded envy our enemies strike out, because they've lost their place of honor and it now belongs to us. Again, Jesus says in John's gospel:

> *"You did not choose me, but I chose you and appointed you to go and bear fruit—fruit that will last." John 15:16*
>
> *"As it is, you do not belong to the world, but I have chosen you out of the world. That is why the world hates you." John 15:19*

The truth of the gospel lies within the mouth of the true church of Jesus Christ, and that voice is not appealing to the demonic hordes bent on destroying the presence of the church in this age. But we can take heart, Jesus said that he would build his church and *"the gates of hell will not overcome it." Matt. 16:18*

It's important to remember that if we desire to reign with him, that we are prepared to endure with him. *(II Tim. 2:12)*

It's all part of the package deal when we're family members with Christ. To the saints at Rome Paul said:

> *"Now if we are children, then we are heirs—heirs of God and co-heirs with Christ, if indeed we share in his sufferings in order that we may share in his glory. I consider that our present sufferings are not worth comparing with the glory that will be revealed in us."* Rom. 8:17–18

## A BRIEF HISTORY OF THE PERSECUTED CHURCH

I've often said that one of the necessities for every believer should be at least an overall understanding of the history of the Christian church. Without it, we fail to appreciate all the efforts taken by those before us, and what their part of knowing the truth provided for us. It's our spiritual ancestry if you will, and in reality, we are more connected to those who did the will of God before us than many of our family members who don't care about advancing the truth.

Of course, this history should begin with a good grasp on the Book of Acts, which reveals common patterns seen throughout the rest of church history right up to the day we live in.

After the death of the last of the first apostles, near the end of the first century, the church entered into a period of history known as, "the early church fathers". These were leaders who were direct disciples of one of the original 12 apostles—like Ignatius, who was a direct disciple of John, or Papias, who directly followed Ignatius. These men and many others form a "chain of custody" that linked their generation to the previous one.

We have a record of many of their writings to this day, and they used the previous letters from the NT to teach and instruct their congregations at that time. The early church fathers always confirmed everything about the NT accounts and the gospels of Christ's life and ministry. It's been said that the entire NT can be reconstructed from the quotes of the early church fathers, with the exception of eleven verses!

It's not the focus of this book to elaborate in much detail about that time or the centuries that followed. *What is* very apparent through the first 400 years, and then to follow, is that the persecution of the true church has never ceased. It's continued to spread to every nation that has heard the gospel. And in many cases very violently and with much blood shed.

A picture of this persecution is seen when John describes the dragon's warfare against the saints in Rev. 12:17:

> *"Then the dragon was enraged at the woman and went off to make war against the rest of her offspring—those who obey God's commandments and hold to the testimony of Jesus."*

The dragon was unable to keep the woman, (Israel), from bringing forth the promised man child who is destined to rule all nations. Since the resurrection of Christ, satan's strategy is to take it out on the rest of the family members—that's everyone who has sincerely given their lives to Christ.

He works very frequently and methodically through earthly governments that are oppressive and filled with control freaks.

The more tolerant a government is, generally the more freedom the church has in spreading the gospel. The more oppressive a government is, the more restricted the church is in openly sharing the gospel message. This has been true throughout church history even to this day. All of this is likewise predicted in the book of Revelation, which obviously confirms the words of Christ.

According to *Halley's Bible Handbook*, during the first 400 years of persecution against the church, Christians sought refuge in the catacombs under Rome. This extensive cave system became a burial ground for millions of believers trying to escape the persecution of Imperial Rome. It is estimated that between 3.5 to 4 million are buried there, and more than 4,000 inscriptions have been found belonging to the period between Tiberius and Constantine. [Note 1]

During the reign of Innocent III (1198–1216), he instituted what is known as the Inquisition. This was developed by the Roman Catholic Church at a time when they were horribly corrupt and influenced by the antichrist spirit. It was a church court to detect and punish heretics in many European countries, through various means of imprisonment, burnings, and confiscation of personal property. If you were against the policies of the Roman Church you were considered a heretic.

Later on, the Inquisition was the main agency in the Papal's effort to crush the Reformation. It is stated that in the 30 years between 1540 and 1570 no fewer than 900,000 Protestants were put to death in the Pope's war for the extermination of the Waldenses, a large group in southern France who taught the Bible as the sole rule for belief and life. [Note 2]

Most recently, the nation of Nigeria has seen Christians there facing a demonic attack through Islamic extremists. As reported in a Fox news article , *"Jihadists organizations, including Boko Haram, have exercised religiously implicated killings over the last 16 years, massacring 125,000 Christians and over 60,000 "liberal" Muslims who do not share the extremist views of the prevailing groups. In that time, 19,000 churches have been sacked. Now, according to Open Doors, more Christians are killed for their faith in Nigeria than anywhere else in the world combined, even though Nigeria is seventh out of the top 50 countries known for persecution of Christians."* [Note 3]

If this is not considered great tribulation, then I don't know what is. While I certainly don't wish increasing persecution on any Christian group, I think it's a very misguided notion to think that millions of believers will be "raptured" away to escape increasingly difficult times of persecution. As I stated in the previous chapter, the reason for the rapture is not to provide a defensive maneuver to escape the tribulation. It's to prepare us with a new body for the new earth, which is our inheritance and new home.

## WHO ARE THOSE IN GREAT TRIBULATION?

> *"After this I looked and there before me was a great multitude that no one could count from every nation, tribe, people and language, standing before the throne and in front of the Lamb. They were wearing white robes and were holding palm branches in their hands." Rev. 7:9*

> *"Then one of the elders asked me, 'These in white robes—who are they, and where did they come from?'*

*I answered, 'Sir, you know.' And he said, 'Theses are they who have come out of great tribulation; they have washed their robes and made them white in the blood of the Lamb." Rev. 7:13–14*

Those who hold the future view of the end times, see the great tribulation as something that takes place over a literal seven year period of time, yet future. But what the church has faced in its history cannot possibly be seen as anything less than great tribulation. To think otherwise is to deny the facts that are in the news everyday. Nothing could be a greater tribulation than the persecution and death already experienced by thousands who have refused to compromise their faith in Christ. This is great distress and pressure like the early church faced.

If the rapture occurs *before* a great tribulation of seven years, then who are those "left behind", and being persecuted and coming out of this great tribulation? Some people think it's the carnal and lukewarm Christians left behind. That's ridiculous—all of us are saved *and kept* by grace! Thankfully, the blood of Christ was factored in to cover all of your mistakes when God said, "I think you should grow up." Nothing you are struggling with is going to keep you here when the archangel blows the last trumpet, and that's the day it's all over. Everything changes at that point.

Still others claim that the church is not even mentioned after the opening verse of Revelation chapter 4. What they overlook is that the church is described by many different names, and seen in many different images throughout the NT. Here are just a few that you'll recognize: The little flock, *(John 10:16)*, imitators of God, *(Eph.5:1)*, the bride of Christ, *(Eph.5:27,32)*, a soldier, *(Eph.6:13–17)*, an athlete, *(I Cor.9:24)*. On and on we could go.

When you read how Peter describes the church, and compare it with John's description of the people of God in the book of Revelation, it's obvious they are both writing about the same group of people—the church.

> *"But you are a chosen people, a royal priesthood, a holy nation, a people belonging to God ..." I Pet. 2:9*

John opens his letter in Rev. 1:6, by saying, *"to him who loves us and has freed us from our sins by his blood, and has made us to be a kingdom and priests ..."* He continues in chapter 5 by saying: *"... you were slain, and with your blood you purchased men for God from every tribe and language and people and nation. You have made them to be a kingdom and priests to serve our God and they will reign on the earth." Rev. 5:9–10*

This is just one of many examples of how the church is described and seen throughout the book of Revelation.

## WHO DO THE 144,000 REPRESENT?

Another beautiful picture we have of the church in the book of Revelation is the 144,000 mentioned in *Rev. 7:1–8, and 14:1–5*. Those who come out of the great tribulation are the same ones sealed earlier in the chapter—the 144,000. Those who come out of the great tribulation are so great a number that John cannot attempt to count them, but they are represented by this group of 144,000. This is just one of many pictures and images of the church throughout the book of Revelation.

Here, in the United States, we have 435 members in the House of Representatives who represent the entire population of Americans, some 330 million people. The representatives are a symbolic numbered group that represent the entire number of Americans.

This is the same idea here with the 144,000. They represent the entire number of Christians for all time, which John saw as a group so large he couldn't number them. That the number is highly symbolic of the church should not be that hard to see when you stop to consider how symbolic these numbers are, and how they're used in Scripture.

Some future view teachers try to interpret Revelation in a very literal sense. They think the 144,000 are actually virgin male Jews which are especially sealed during a future time of Revelation. *(Rev.14:3–4)* Wow, good luck finding that. I'm not sure you could find that many virgins in this generation! Let's look at it a different way.

**Why is it exactly 144,000?** God can count. It's not 143,581, or 145,346. It's a specific number that just "so happens" to be divisible and broken down into other numbers that are highly symbolic in scripture. Like 12 times 1,000. Those seem familiar in a number of ways: There were 12 tribes that represented the full number of the people of Israel. There are 12 apostles that represent the fullness of the NT people. The heavenly Jerusalem has 12 gates made out of 12 pearls. *(See Rev. 21)* There are 24 elders (12 x 2) seated around God's throne. *(Rev. 4:4)*

Additionally, each tribe is numbered with the same identical number each time—12 x 1,000.

What's the likelihood that 12 different groups would actually total the same exact number?

**Why is the number 1,000 used?** Psalm 50:10 declares that God owns the cattle on a thousand hills. I'm sure you realize his ownership is greater than 1,000 hills. The psalmist is expressing an idea, not literally, but figuratively.

*II Pet.3:8 "… With the Lord a day is like a thousand years, and a thousand years are like a day."* Peter could have said a day with the Lord is like 10,000 years. It would still be true.

*Rev. 5:11 "Then I looked and heard the voice of many angels, numbering thousands upon thousands, and ten thousand times ten thousand."*

Again, the writer is not focusing on a specific number—he's trying to convey the idea of an expansive kingdom, and a seemingly never ending number.

**Why is the tribe of Judah listed first?** This is very significant in its listed order and tells us once again that the list is symbolic and represents a much larger group. In the OT listing of the 12 tribes of Israel, most of the time they are listed it starts with the tribe of Reuben first, because he was Jacob's first-born. The only time the list order differs is when the passage is emphasizing a tribe for some specific function—like the tribe of Levi that's singled out for the priesthood. Chronicles list the tribe of Judah first, because when the Jews returned from captivity, they held to the promise that the line of David would have an enduring dynasty, which of course is only fulfilled through Christ.

Judah is listed here first, because the emphasis in Revelation is on Jesus, who not only is promised an enduring dynasty, but is revealed to be the Lion of the tribe of Judah.

*"See, the lion of the tribe of Judah, the Root of David, has triumphed. He is able to open the scroll and it's seven seals." Rev. 5:5.*

We're told earlier in *Rev. 2:26–27* that the overcoming saints are promised to be joint-heirs with Christ and to partner with him in his rulership.

> *"To him that overcomes and does my will to the end, I will give authority over the nations—He will rule them with an iron scepter; he will dash them to pieces like pottery—just as I have received authority from my Father."*

**Why does the "sealing" appear as if it's for the 12 tribes of Israel?** Because of God's grace and divine election, the nation of Israel was chosen as his special people. When they walked in faith and obedience before the Lord, there was nothing, or anyone, that could stop them from possessing all that God had for them.

God wants us to recognize that just as Israel was a special people sealed and secure in his love, so we in the body of Christ, made up of Jew and Gentile alike, are just as special and just as sealed.

> *"Having believed, you were marked in him with a seal, the promised Holy Spirit, who is a deposit guaranteeing our inheritance until the redemption of those who are God's possession—to the praise of his glory." Eph. 1:13–14*

## OVERCOMING GREAT TRIBULATION

All of these groups are pictures and representations of the church from God's perspective. Each picture and the details are meant to convey an image of absolute overcoming, even if it means actual death on our part. A familiar passage is *Rev.12:11:*

*"They overcame him by the blood of the Lamb and by the word of their testimony; and they did not love their lives so much as to shrink from death."*

This really echoes Paul's experience when he encourages the church at Rome when facing great tribulation and distress. He asks them:

> *"Who shall separate us from the love of Christ? Shall trouble or hardship or persecution or famine or nakedness or danger or sword? As it is written: For your sake we face death all day long; we are considered as sheep to be slaughtered. No, in all these things we are more than conquerors through him who loved us." Rom. 8:35–37*

I'm not implying that the only way to overcome this is to die a martyr's death. Most of us should just start with the same commitment Paul had, when he said, *"I die daily."*

That's a big enough commitment for a lot of people. But if we find it near impossible to live an unselfish life, it will be very difficult to imagine laying down our life for our faith in Christ.

It's also important to be aware of the fact that the intensity of tribulation is not always experienced the same throughout history, or from country to country. There are times when freedoms are greater and we should use them to our advantage to get the gospel out, and to support those who are facing a greater trial somewhere else. Hebrews admonishes us to, *"Remember those in prison as if you were their fellow prisoners, and those who are mistreated as if you yourselves were suffering." Hebs. 13:3*

Likewise, there's no rigid answer to deal with intense persecution in the day it may come our way. On at least two occasions Paul used his Roman citizen rights to stay alive and advance the gospel cause. Even shortly after his conversion, his life was threatened to the point that others put him in a large basket and lowered him to the ground on the outside wall of the city. From there he escaped. *(Acts 9:23–25)*

Deliverance may come through the prayers of people like it did for the apostle Peter when Herod planned on killing him. *(Acts 12)* Peter was delivered that time, but church history has strongly held that the end of his life came during the persecution which intensified under the reign of Nero later on. Paul was martyred shortly after that as well.

Whatever level of great trouble and intense distress that the church may face, we can be assured that our risen Savior stands with us, and He will give us the grace to overcome at that time. Like Stephen, we can look up knowing that the fullness of our redemption has come. It becomes an hour for us to shine and to be full of the Holy Spirit and his boldness. *(Acts 7:55–56)*

In the end, there's nothing that can separate us from the love of God that is in Christ Jesus our Lord *(Rom. 8:38–39)*—all of us come out of great tribulation with a faith that is refined like gold in a fire. The dross floats to the top and only the good metal remains. This is the kind of people that God seals for eternity.

# 11

# LIVING IN THE "ALREADY, BUT NOT YET"

**PREVIOUSLY, WE COVERED** how common it is for God's people to face various challenges, and to use their faith to trust God for a way through the troubles and pressures they face. The prophet Daniel lived the majority of his life in a heathen kingdom, Babylon, under one of the most arrogant rulers ever, king Nebuchadnezzar.

Beginning under the kingdom of Babylon, he served where he could, living out a deeply devoted life that never strayed from the internal convictions that, no doubt, were impressed upon him at an early age. *(See Daniel 1)* It seems obvious early on, that God providentially gifted him with amazing abilities and spiritual capacities. *Daniel 1:17–19.* I'm sure right away Daniel figured it was wise to make the best of a bad situation, and not tick off the king.

The overriding theme of the book of Daniel is the ultimate control God has over the nations. He reigns supreme and sovereign over all nations, and He is involved in more than just strengthening his people. He is even able to make the pride of man praise him, such as Nebuchadnezzar, who God actually called, "his servant" in *Jer. 25:9*, and he foreknows all men, just like he did king Cyrus 150 years before he showed up in history. *(Is. 45:13)*

When Daniel interprets the king's dream,*(2:27–44)*, it provides all of us with a revelation of the omni's of God—that God is omniscient, he is omnipresent, and he is omnipotent. Nothing escapes his notice and no event is beyond his capacity to work through—even the kingdoms of men. God is actively working through history even when it appears we are faced with insurmountable difficulties. *Daniel 2:44* becomes the climactic point of the dreams interpretation:

> *"In the time of those kings, the God of heaven will set up a kingdom that will never be destroyed, nor will it be left to another people. It will crush all those other kingdoms and bring them to an end, but it will itself endure forever. This is the meaning of the vision of the rock cut out of a mountain, but not by human hands—a rock that broke the iron, the bronze, the silver and the gold to pieces. The great God has shown the king what will take place in the future." Daniel 2:44–45*

Likewise, the theme we see in the book of Daniel, is largely what is revealed throughout the book of Revelation, plus more. Jesus Christ is revealed as the King of kings, regardless of the kings on the earth. All who side with Christ, will join in his battle against the dark forces who are deceiving mankind. The kingdom of God has come, and continues to grow until it fills the whole earth. *(Rev. 1:5–6; Daniel 2:44; Matt.13:31)* As Isaiah prophesied: "*... the government will be on his shoulders, and of the increase of his government and his peace there will be no end." Is. 9:6–7*

Its interesting to note that so much of what Daniel saw, he was told to *"seal up the words". (Daniel 12:4,9)* But when we come to the book of Revelation, John is told to declare what he has seen, because the Lion of the tribe of Judah, Jesus, is worthy to open the seals. *(Rev. 5:1–5)*

## THE "ALREADY, BUT NOT YET" KINGDOM

In the 7th chapter of Daniel, the prophet is given his own vision that grants him insight into the next 500 years of history, the same as the dream the king had previously had in Daniel 2. However, this dream extends far beyond the changing of human empires. Here, we are introduced to what all of us must learn. It's what's commonly referred to as the "already, but not yet". The kingdom of God has already arrived, but its fullness is not yet complete.

Reading from *Daniel 7:16–18* we're told: *"I approached one of those standing there and asked him the true meaning of all this. So he told me and gave me the interpretation of these things. The four great beasts are four kingdoms that will rise from the earth. But the saints of the Most High will receive the kingdom and will possess it forever—yes, forever and ever."*

Of course, we have to come over to the NT side of things to see how all of this will play out, and I'll talk more about that shortly, but at the moment you should know that the kingdom of God will be opposed by the prince of darkness and his legions.

This is shown to Daniel three different times in the vision. Here are the three references:

> *"I kept looking until the beast was slain and its body destroyed and thrown into the blazing fire. (The other beasts had been stripped of their authority, but were allowed to live for a period of time.)". Daniel 7:11–12*

> *"As I watched, this horn was waging war against the saints and defeating them, until the Ancient of Days came and pronounced judgment in favor of the saints of the Most High, and the time came when they possessed the kingdom." Daniel 7:21–22*

> *"But the courts will sit, and his power will be taken away and completely destroyed forever. Then the sovereignty, power and greatness of the kingdom under the whole heaven will be handed over to the saints, the people of the Most High. His kingdom will be an everlasting kingdom, and all rulers will worship and obey him." Daniel 7:26–27*

**Two things become very clear:** The kingdom of God will endure and overcome everything, but in the meantime the saints must endure and stand against the opposition.

## THE KINGDOM ADVANCES FACING OPPOSITION

The various beasts in Daniel represent human governments

that try to oppress and control the people of the Most High. What is introduced in Daniel, is amplified and exposed in a greater way in the book Revelation. In Revelation chapter 13, you can hear echoes of what was shown to Daniel previously:

> *"Men worshipped the dragon because he had given authority to the beast, and they also worshiped the beast and asked, "Who is like the beast? Who can wage war against him?"*
>
> *The beast was given a mouth to utter proud words and blasphemies and to exercise his authority for 42 months. He opened his mouth to blaspheme God, and to slander his name and his dwelling place and those who live in heaven. He was given power to make war against the saints and to conquer them." Rev. 13:4–7*

As a result of this opposition, John tells his readers in verse 10: *"This calls for patient endurance and faithfulness on the part of the saints." Rev. 13:10*

Again, this should not be taken to assume it's a selected time in the future of 42 literal months; it's meant to symbolize the strategy of the evil powers to try to oppose the saints ever since the dragon was defeated. An early preview of this is seen when the Christ child is born. We're told that *"the dragon stood in front of the woman who was about to give birth, so that he might devour the child the moment it was born." Rev. 12:4*. This dragon was the real influence behind the actions of king Herod. *(Matt. 2:14–16)*

Later, when Jesus begins his public ministry, the adversary

is defeated on every occasion and at every turn—he's never able to get the upper hand on Christ. At the last supper, Jesus could tell his disciples that the prince of this world had tried to shake him, but there was no open door into the life of Christ. *(John 14:30)* The apostle John would summarize Jesus' appearance by saying: *"The reason the Son of God appeared was to destroy the devil's work." I John 3:8*

The opposition works both ways. Satan is opposing Christ and the kingdom of God. Likewise, Christ is opposing the kingdom of darkness by casting out every kind of spirit, and declaring that every kind of darkness is subject to the Spirit of the living God! *(Matt. 12:28)* Until Jesus was ready to lay down his life for humanity, nobody was able to take his life from him—neither man, demon, or ruler of any kind. *(John 10:17–18)*

To prove that his kingdom was greater and more permanent, he gave the authority he had to his disciples, and commissioned them to do the same things he did. They clearly had the same results and came back rejoicing about it. *(Luke 10:17)* Because Christ was willing to humble himself to the lowest point of death, even death on a cross, God has exalted him to the highest place and given him the name that is above every name." *(Phil. 2:8–9)*

Passages like this, and dozens more, underscore the present truth that we live in a kingdom that is already here, and moving toward full completion. Our adversary has already been defeated at the cross and by the power of the resurrection. The dragon has been convicted and found guilty, but not yet sentenced and put into final prison. *(Rev. 20:10)* In the meantime, he's opposed to the kingdom of God, and we're opposed to him.

The present battle shows why he is guilty and destined to the lake of fire. His character has never changed, and those who follow him never do either, unless they turn to Christ completely. *(John 8:44; I John 3:8)* Peter writing to the church gives us our marching orders in his first letter: *"Be self-controlled and alert. Your enemy the devil prowls around like a roaring lion looking for someone to devour. Resist him, standing firm in the faith, because you know that your brothers throughout the world are undergoing the same kind of sufferings." I Pet. 5:8–9.*

The question naturally comes up: If the enemy's defeated why not remove him completely now? At the present time, he and all who follow him are showing their true colors and proving why the justice of God is true and righteous. Along with that, this is our hour to prove that we're overcomers, and that the life and death of Christ was not in vain. God knows you're an overcomer, but you don't know you're an overcomer until you prove it to yourself by fighting the good fight of faith. *(I Tim. 6:12; I John 5:4)*

We win because we're destined to win, and we overcome by the blood of the Lamb, and the word of our testimony, and if necessary, even to the point of not loving our lives unto death. *(Rev. 12:11)* You may not be able to keep the enemy out of the lives of others, but you sure can keep him out of your own life! So, stand, resist, and overcome!

## THE KINGDOM OF GOD IS DESIGNED TO GROW

When we turn to the kingdom of God and humbly receive our king, whether we know it or not, we receive an inheritance that is beyond our wildest imaginations. For most of us, it takes a lifetime to grasp the magnitude of it and appreciate how expansive it can really be. As a child of God and a citizen of the kingdom, all of the benefits and the responsibilities included in your inheritance are all yours, as well as the opposition and the persecution too! *(John 16:33; II Pet. 1:3–4)*

Jesus never saw his church as a bunch of spiritual beggars unable to stand, or too dumb to attain the principles of his kingdom. He promised the power to do the works he did, and a divine Helper to reveal the secrets of his kingdom. We are not left as orphans and victims of our past. *(John 14:12; 14:16–17; 16:12–13)* Like Isaiah prophesied, the Lord proclaims an ever increasing kingdom that will know no end *(Is. 9:6)*, and a church strong enough that the gates of hell cannot prevail against it. *(Matt. 16:18)*

One of the days when Jesus taught, he focused on the ever increasing growth of the kingdom of God. He showed how the kingdom of God affects the inside of you, how it affects the corporate body of Christ, the church, and the impact of the kingdom of God on the whole world by the end of time. *(Matt. 13; Mark 4)*

**Consider the basic meaning of the parables Jesus taught that day**

- Parable of the *sower* – Sowing God's word into your life brings growth & good fruit
- Parable of the *tares & wheat* – The kingdom will grow during every age until Christ returns
- Parable of the *mustard seed* – The kingdom starts extremely small but will influence the whole earth by the time its done growing

- Parable of the *leaven* – The kingdom will experience extensive transformation for growth
- Parable of *unconscious growth* – Doing the common things, uncommonly well, brings growth
- Parable of the *hidden treasure & the fine pearl* – The sacrifices you make to gain the kingdom are rewarded with fruitful change and growth.
- Parable of the *dragnet* – When Christ returns evil is separated out, and those who have remained true will inherit the full growth of the kingdom at that time.

The one constant element of each of these parables is growth. It's not stagnation, not decline, not escaping, not growing outdated, or looking dull and dead—it is growth.

Let's keep the growing going!

## WORLDWIDE CHURCH GROWTH BY THE NUMBERS

If you listen to the voice of the false prophet, which is today's media, you get the idea that the church is irrelevant, it's in decline, and doomed to either go underground, or hide up in the hills until Christ secretly returns to bail us all out of here. Nothing could be further from the truth. Despite the forces of the antichrist spirit opposing it, and in spite of its own mistakes, the church continues to grow and advance to this present hour.

Below are some encouraging statistics gathered by missiologists, (people that study missions), that were calculated up to five years ago, 2019. Since that time, the percentages will no doubt be higher.

*The best estimates of the Christian population by A.D. 100, against the probable world population of about 250 million, was one believer for every 360 people.* Note 1

By A.D. 1430—One out of every 99

By A.D. 1790—One out of every 49

By A.D. 1940—One out of every 32

By A.D. 1960—One out of every 24

By A.D. 1970—One out of every 19

By A.D. 1980—One out of every 16

By A.D. 1989—One out of every 10

By A.D. 1995—One out of every 8

*In practical, down to earth terms, this means "there are 78,000 conversions each day and 16,000 new churches planted each week."* Note 2

*The Prayer Foundation shares some amazing statistics, along with some serious needs*

> *The number of Christians in Indonesia has grown from 1.3 million 40 years ago to over 11 million today, although out of 76,000 villages, 50,000 are without a church. (Operation World)*
>
> *Wycliffe's Bible Translators believes it will have a Bible translation for every people group by 2042. This has been accelerated by 100 years. (Wycliffe's Vision 2025)*

*The Jesus Film has been translated into nearly 1,000 languages and over 200 million people have made decisions for Christ as a result of the film. (Campus Crusade)*

*About 500 Muslims come to faith in Christ every month in Iran—a country ranked among the top ten persecutors of Christians in the world. Many of the new believers are young, since 70 percent of Iran is under the age of 30.*

*Every day 20,000 Africans come to Christ. Africa is now over 50 percent Christian. (Vision 2020)*

*In 1900 Korea had no Protestant church and the country was deemed impenetrable. Today Korea is 30 percent Christian with 7,000 churches in Seoul alone, and several of these churches have over 1 million members. (Vision 2020)*

*There are currently approx. 80 million Christians in China, with between 10,000 to 25,000 converts a day. (Open Doors)* [Note 3]

Other mission groups report statistics that are very agreeable to these findings. What this shows is a church that has boldly moved forward, and not caved into the dragon's intimidation. The ministry of the Holy Spirit is very much alive and active in drawing the multitudes to Christ. He has never left the church and he will continue to empower it until the last trumpet is blown and Christ returns!

In the meantime, there are millions of new believers who are young in the faith, and need a lot of help being discipled and strengthened to achieve all that God has for them. Jesus commissioned us to go into all nations and make disciples. People cannot be discipled until they've been converted to the true faith, but having received the grace of salvation, they will need to start feeding on the milk of God's word to keep growing. *(I Pet. 2:2)* So, there's a lot more equipping needed to help people mature in Christ. *(Eph. 4:13–15)*

## YOUR PRAYERS CAN HELP CHANGE HISTORY

I don't think anybody would deny the fact that the prophet Daniel had a dedicated prayer life. We're told that he prayed three times a day worshiping God and seeking God's help regardless of who was in power or ruling at that time. *(Daniel 6:10–13)* *Daniel 5:12* tells us that Daniel had a keen mind and knowledge and understanding, and the ability to interpret dreams and solve difficult problems.

There's a definite pattern where it appears that Daniel's prayer life led to the revelations given to him, and the revelations given to Daniel caused him to pray with much fervency about the matter. *(Daniel 9)* Prayer brought revelation and revelation brought prayer. But Daniel is not called to this task alone. He served the purposes of God in his generation, and God has called us to do the same in our generation.

When the disciples watched Jesus praying, I'm sure at some point they made the connection between his consistent prayer life and the successful public ministry he always had. So, they came and asked the Lord to teach them to pray, just as John had taught his disciples. *(Luke 11:1)* Here, we learn that prayer is involved in carrying out the will of God in the earth, the same as his will is expressed in heaven. *(Matt. 6:10)*

We can do more after we've prayed, but prayer becomes the

foundation for everything else. Christ is not only standing in the presence of God for us, but he has instructed us to pray with the authority that is found in his name. *(John 16:23–24)* There is no name that is greater than the name of Jesus, and when we express it in prayer, that is based on the word of God, we are standing in full assurance that he can and will bring change. It may not happen when we think, or how we think, but we can be assured that the answer is on it's way, the same as Daniel during the 21 days he prayed. *(Daniel 10:2,12–13)*

## YOU HAVE KINGDOM AUTHORITY—WHAT IT MEANS FOR YOU

We don't have authority over human wills or human spirits, but we do have authority over demonic spirits. This authority was transferred to us when Christ was raised from the dead and given a name above every other name. *(Phil. 2:9)* What you don't know can hurt you when it comes to spiritual things. The keys to bind and loose have been given to the church, but if the church doesn't know what belongs to them, then they can suffer in many ways for a lot longer than necessary because they're not using what Jesus gave them. We have to ask ourselves, if the church prayed with the same commitment and intensity that Daniel showed, would more situations and circumstances change? I think so.

The responsibility and authority go hand in hand. To be given responsibility without authority, is like a policeman given the responsibility to keep the roads safe, but not the authority to fine those who are acting in an unsafe manner on the roads. The church has the responsibility to go into all the world and take the gospel message to all nations, and make disciples as well. Because we have the responsibility, we have the authority to establish God's will and his word, because Christ gave it to the church when he departed. *(Matt. 28:18–19)*

I'm not implying that it will be easy or simply done in one night, but God's word is very clear that if you want freedom you must be willing to fight for it. And the biggest war for most people is the one between their two ears—especially when it comes to fighting for what is ours in Christ. The authority that Christ has already given his church is probably the most overlooked revelation that we have been given. Our success rises and falls on what we know about that and how we use it.

## FAITH MAKES PRAYER WORK

The reality of change is all around us, but the potential for good change is found when we exercise our faith based on the promises of God. The promises of God are backed by the character of God and He declares repeatedly that he is faithful and watches over his word to perform it. *(Jer. 1:12)* Let's consider for a moment what Jesus taught us beginning in *Luke 18:1:*

> *"Then Jesus told his disciples a parable to* ***show them that they should always pray and not give up.*** *He said: "In a certain town there was a judge who neither feared God nor cared about men. And there was a widow in that town who kept coming to him with the plea, 'Grant me justice against my adversary.' For some time he refused. But finally he said to himself, 'Even though I don't fear God or care about men, yet because this widow keeps*

*bothering me, I will see that she gets justice, so that she won't eventually wear me out with her coming!'*

*And the Lord said, "Listen to what the unjust judge says, And will not God bring about justice for his chosen ones, who cry out to him day and night? Will he keep putting them off? I tell you, he will see that they get justice, and quickly.*

*However,* ***when the Son of Man comes will he find faith on the earth?"*** *Luke 18:1–8*

This is such a powerful message on so many levels. God works in cooperation with the church to accomplish his will, because he has given the church the responsibility to bring about change through prayer. The unjust judge is to be *contrasted* to God, not *compared* to God. The unjust judge finally dealt with the widow's adversary because he was tired of hearing her whine about the problem. She was no longer able to bring about change. God doesn't answer us because we wear him down, but because we continue to exercise faith even when we're faced with circumstances that look contrary.

The praying church is the change agent that God uses to bring about change in history—both in your family and in your nation. I don't know what your nation may face in the future, but I'm sure there is a God who cares about it, and invites you to help change the course of things by praying and exercising faith and authority in the name of Jesus! Each of us must answer the Lord's question ourselves: When the Son of Man comes will he find faith on the earth?

Jesus taught all of us this lesson, because he knew there would be times when we would feel like giving up. We're not seeing change, the problem looks like it's growing bigger, I'm not sure God is listening to me right now, etc. etc. This is why prayer must be accompanied with faith, based on what we know to be God's revealed will. Clearly, Jesus is telling us here, that he expects us to trust him for change and not throw our hands up in the air, and talk the language of doubt and unbelief.

God is in the circumstance changing business, and even if you cannot change everything for everybody, God wants to use you to bring about change for somebody! God's word reveals that prayer is involved with any good changes that happen. When Jesus gave us the great commission, he gave us the prayer commission as well. He was reaching out to us, and in effect saying, "tag, you're it."

One day the Lord came to the patriarch Abraham's house *(how would you like that?).* The Lord told him that the stench of the sin of Sodom and Gomorrah was so great that he would have to destroy it. By this time Abraham knows that God doesn't destroy the righteous with the wicked, and he knows his nephew Lot is a citizen of Sodom—he even sits on the city council. In a beautiful picture of the long-suffering of God, Abraham works his petition down to ten righteous people—that would be enough to stall judgment and save the two towns. *(I guess Abraham thought there would be at least ten people he could count on!) (See Gen.18)*

Of course we know the outcome of the story—the towns could not be spared from judgment. What we do need to see is that the prayers of intercession Abraham made for Lot, gave Lot and his family the opportunity to be spared from judgment. *(Gen. 19:29)*

Even his future son in laws could have escaped the destruction but they thought Lot was just joking about all of it! *(Gen. 19:12)*

## PRAYING FOR THOSE IN AUTHORITY & HIGH POSITIONS

We live in a time when there are over 195 nations in the world. The freedoms and the restrictions in these countries vary from one to another, but as a common observation, the greater the religious freedom, the greater the true liberty the nation has. If the nation has many restrictions, either religious or secular, the personal freedoms are restricted more as well.

I can't give an acceptable answer as to why some restrictions, in some countries, last as long as they do. But I know biblical history and world history shows that change can come and that prayer is almost certainly involved in it. The early church was persecuted intensely for the first three hundred years, and then Christianity was lawfully accepted and the persecution dwindled, or moved to another area.

During that time, leaders were instructed to pray for kings and all those in authority. It is clearly God's will for men to be saved and the gospel to be spread with the resulting peace that follows. *(I Tim. 2:1–4)* But as we know, there is always a tension between the will of God being made known and the will of God being received and acted upon. During this time of tension, the saints must continue to pray and trust that the Holy Spirit is massaging and softening hearts, convicting them to turn from their evil ways. *(John 16:8–10)*

If you live in a nation that permits Christian freedoms, you would be foolish not to take advantage of them to further the gospel in any way possible, from the voting booth to the city council, to the church pulpit. On at least two occasions, the apostle Paul used his rights as a Roman citizen to further the gospel and avoid greater persecution. *(See Acts 16:37; 23:16–23)* I think wisdom would call us to do the same.

The early church started in a city and a nation that was highly religious, but very restrictive when it came to hearing the news of the risen Christ. It was not a popular position to be in when they started out. They were threatened and put in jail, and told to stop spreading the gospel. But what did Peter and John do— *"On their release, Peter and John went back to their own people and reported all that the chief priests and elders had said to them. When they heard this, they raised their voices together in prayer to God." (Acts 4:23–24)*

They didn't pray for a way out. They prayed for a greater boldness and that God's healing power would be even greater to exalt the name of Jesus. And as all of them prayed, God answered their prayer, and filled them with the Holy Spirit and the boldness to continue proclaiming the name of Jesus. *(Acts 4:29–31)*

> *For 45 years all of Eastern Europe lived under the oppression of the Iron Curtain; the communist ideology that restricted freedoms throughout Eastern Europe after WW2.*
>
> *A group of believers got ahold of a book that was printed in West Germany and smuggled into Eastern Germany, which was communist at the time. The book, The Believers Authority, revealed to them the authority they had to pray for their nation and about their government. Up until that time, they spent their time griping and complaining*

*about the oppression they lived under.*

*They began to dedicate themselves to the kind of prayer that would change their nation and overthrow the oppressive governments. Within a short time, God orchestrated events where their prayers were answered and the walls came down, and Eastern Europe has enjoyed a freedom for the past 35 years that they didn't have before. Praise God!* **Note 4**

## WHAT COULD STILL BE AHEAD FOR THE CHURCH ?

I hope you understand from this chapter some of the issues we are dealing with. The enemy will bring the fight to you, but we can overcome with the fundamental tools God has given us—authority as believers to use the name of Jesus, faith based on his revealed word, and expressed through prayer and endurance. These are foundational for the fight.

God will never let his program and plan be snuffed out by renegade fallen angels who are destined for hell. His love will continue to reach out to a wayward society, and I believe the Holy Spirit will continue to move and bring a visitation to this generation. I think the past number of harvests prove to us that another harvest is right around the corner, and as a praying church we should prepare for it.

Even though the spirit of the antichrist is growing and persecution still exists, we should pray that God continues to hold a restraining hand over evil, until the full number of those appointed to eternal life make their decision. Because no man knows the day or the hour, it is possible that this is the final generation. Maybe, maybe not.

I think one verse that provides us with a possible timeline is Matt. 24:14 which says:

*And this gospel of the kingdom will be preached in the whole world as a testimony to all nations, and then the end will come." Matt.24:14*

Only God can define what the fullness of the testimony should be. Until then, let's continue to gather in the harvest at hand!

# 12

# KEYS TO INTERPRETING THE BOOK OF REVELATION

THE SCOPE OF this book is not meant to be an exposition of the book of Revelation. I simply want to share what I've discovered that has helped me, and encourage all of us to realize there is more to learn than what we have learned up to this point. If you have only heard one view up till now, and if you have heard it intensely, then I encourage you to make a decision to not read *into* the text; instead, let the context read *out to you.*

I spent eight years hearing and seeing primarily one view, and I had already studied and taught Biblical prophecy to others from the one view I had learned about. When the eyes of my understanding were opened, I realized there were a lot of prophecy issues I needed to "unlearn". The Holy Spirit helped me to see things differently and more clearly, the same as he has done with other passages in the NT, and on other subjects. So, as I mentioned previously, there can be a lot of sincerity from others, but still be sincerely wrong.

To gain a better understanding of Revelation, the first

guideline is to realize it's a distinct kind of literature called apocalyptic, which is highly symbolic. This is not a literature that is very common in the Western world, but the book gives us some clues right away that help establish it as a message that's highly symbolic—from start to finish.

The book of Revelation is not the first book in the Bible that has a lot of symbolism in it. Books like Genesis, Exodus, Daniel, and many prophetic passages use a lot of symbolism. Symbolism is frequently seen in dreams and visions. Someone has said that dreams are the "forgotten picture language" of the Holy Spirit.

**Revelation cannot be interpreted chronologically—why not?**

> **In chapter 1,** Christ is walking through the seven churches as the risen Lord and the Head of each local church. This is clearly much later than his resurrection.
>
> **In chapter 4 & 5,** He is the Lamb that was slain, who alone is worthy to open the seals. This period represents the time immediately after his crucifixion and resurrection.
>
> **In chapter 12,** He's the baby that the dragon tried to kill. He's the man child born to the woman (Israel), He's the anointed ruler destined to rule all nations. He's the Victor over all the powers of darkness—both in the past and the present. This chapter covers many different spans of time—it cannot be nailed down to any one time span. Because of arrangements like this, Revelation doesn't specifically predict any historical event at any particular time—not in seven years or seven hundred, or even seven thousand.

**Revelation cannot be interpreted *literally* in most senses—why not?**

That would mean the two edged sword coming from the mouth of Christ is literal, and there would be no reason to use statements that emphasize comparison, like we see John use describing Jesus in *Rev.1:14–16.* Such statements as,

> *"His head and hair were white **like** wool"*
>
> *"His eyes were **like** burning fire"*
>
> *"His feet were **like** bronze glowing in a furnace"*
>
> *"His voice was **like** the sound of rushing waters"*

In each of these cases, John is looking for words that can convey to his readers the powerful impact the appearance of Christ made on him. They were not there to see Christ revealed as John saw him, so John is using terms that his readers can best relate to, and hopefully "see" what John saw.

**For the most part, Revelation should be interpreted *symbolically*.**

It's introduced right away as a book filled with symbolism—that doesn't mean it's fictional or "make believe". The events in Revelation will *literally* happen in some fashion or another, but the *interpretation* of the image and picture conveyed is not intended to be interpreted literally. Symbolically is a much better fit.

*Consider Rev. 1:20:* The seven lamp stands are the seven churches—until this was said, it appeared as a mystery to John.

An early example of symbolism would be in the dreams that Joseph had in *Genesis 37:5–11*. We know that the dream and what Joseph saw was not the important thing, and certainly not to be taken literally. It was the interpretation and what the symbolism meant that counted. The sheaves bowing down to the single sheave misses the point. What it represented was Joseph's brothers eventually submitting to his leadership, that's what the dream was trying to get over to them. How Joseph *handled* his dream is a different topic.

We seem to forget this about symbolism when it comes to understanding the message of Revelation. Example: *Rev. 9:9*—some modern interpreters suggest the locusts represent modern helicopters fitted for war. It's much deeper than that and requires a spiritual understanding. Let's see how the apostle Paul instructed the church at Corinth in regard to spiritual things.

> *"This is what we speak, not in words taught us by human wisdom but in words taught by the Spirit, expressing spiritual truths in spiritual words. The man without the Spirit does not accept the things that come from the Spirit of God, for they are foolishness to him, and he cannot understand them, because they are spiritually discerned."*
> *I Cor. 2:13–14*

This was the problem Nicodemus had when he talked to Jesus about understanding the new birth. *John 3:4*

**Jesus frequently used symbolism when he taught his disciples. Some examples:**

*"Be careful, Jesus said to them. Be on your guard against the yeast of the Pharisees and the Sadducees." They discussed this among themselves and said, "It is because we didn't bring any bread." Aware*

*of their discussion, Jesus asked, "… How is it you don't understand that I was not talking to you about bread? … But be on your guard against the yeast of the Pharisees and Sadducees." Then they understood that he was not telling them to guard against yeast used in bread, but against the teaching of the Pharisees and Sadducees. (Matt. 16:6–8, 11–12)*

*Matt. 16:2–4; Matt.12:40*—The weather and Jonah were symbolic signs to pay attention to.

*Matt.17:11–13; Luke 1:17; Mal. 4:5*—John symbolized the person of Elijah

*John 2:19–22*—The body of Christ symbolized the temple where God's presence resides

**Understanding the symbolism of the book of Revelation** was one of the first things that helped me see Revelation in a better light. One day I was reading about the seven letters to the seven churches. It dawned on me that there were obviously more than seven churches in Asia Minor, and I'm sure at that time they all could have used a letter of exhortation and encouragement from Jesus in regard to the issues they faced. Of course, the passages themselves end with the statement, *"He that has an ear, let him hear what the Spirit says to the churches." Rev. 2:7.* They all end that way.

Each letter had something specific for the church it was originally written to, but the spirit of the message applied to every church—for all time. In this sense, it would be the same as the letter to the Corinthians, or the Ephesians would apply to each of us today. The Holy Spirit of God can make each letter relevant to us today—and He does.

The number seven is used 52 times in Revelation, and the basic idea with the number is that it expresses the idea of *"completion"*. What God wanted to say to the seven churches at that time, and for the time since then, could be said completely through the messages to the seven churches.

These seven churches are not literally here anymore, but they symbolize every kind of church, and I think, every kind of condition that you find churches in today.

In other words, some churches are like the Laodiceans, some are like the church at Smyrna, and some are like the church in Ephesus. And if you've traveled around much in the "church world", you know that this is true!

**The numbers first used in Revelation are symbolic rather than literal.** This sets up a pattern that follows through Revelation and changes how the book gets interpreted. For instance, the term 144,000 can be seen symbolically rather than in a literal fashion (see chapter 10, what I previously covered there).

**Some of the numbers are rounding up, rather than implying a specific number:**

> *Rev. 8:9,12; 9:18*—a third of mankind, a third of the earth, etc.
>
> *Rev. 11:13*—7,000, a number that commonly refers to a large group (cp. *Rom. 11:2–4*).
>
> *Rev. 9:16*—A large number divided evenly by 1,000, which is a number symbolizing expansion and an undetermined amount (cp. *II Pet. 3:8; Ps. 91:7*).

**Some of the different numerical terms used are describing the same thing**

> Times, time, and half a time—*Rev. 12:14 (this matches with Daniel 7:25 for the same period).*
>
> Forty two months—*Rev. 13:5.*
>
> 1,260 days—*Rev. 11:2–3.*
>
> Three and half days—*Rev. 11:9* .

Each of these numbers is symbolizing and/or representing the same idea

> Even a city can symbolize and represent the world—*Rev. 11:8.*

**Revelation doesn't move chronologically through a "one and done" process**

Meaning many of the visions follow the same steps and typically end the same way, with the return of Christ, or some kind of severe judgment. *Compare Rev. 6:12–16; 11:11–13; 16:17–20; 18:19–24; 19:17–21* You'll notice common similarities and common sequences.

**Nothing Jesus says in Revelation is going to contradict what he taught in the gospels**—it's just presented in a different fashion. It's been said that a picture is worth a thousand words, and sometimes a picture, or a vision, is a more graphic way to convey the message. The visions in Revelation are extremely graphic and reveal the depth of what is shown at the very core level—nothing is hidden; the good, the bad, the holy, and the evil.

The characters in Revelation all manifest the same qualities you see elsewhere, and the paradise lost in Genesis, is regained by the end of Revelation.

When you get to the last few chapters of Revelation, chapters 21 & 22, you'll notice that the time references are no longer being used. For example: Times, time, and half a time; or a third of this or that, etc. I think it's because the dimension of time as we know it in this life is no longer needed. You've entered into the eternal state and time references are not needed.

There is no death or decay—the old order of things has passed away. *Rev. 21:4*

**Some thoughts on the "mark of the beast"**

The book of Daniel introduces worldly governments as political entities that not only move through history, but at their worst, they oppress the people of God. Whatever this mark is, it symbolizes the control that various governments try to exercise over the people in their sphere of influence. *Rev. 17*

Every generation of God's people have had to deal with the "beast of government". The threat of worldliness and its encroachment was described by John to the early church, before the warnings about the mark were detailed in Revelation. We're told in I *John 2:15–17:*

> *"Do not love the world or anything in the world. If anyone loves the world, the love of the Father is not in him. For everything in the world- the cravings of sinful man, the lust of his eyes and the boasting of what he does-comes not from the Father but from the world. The world and its*

*desires pass away, but the man who does the will of God lives forever."*

The end result of loving the world, or taking the mark of the beast, is identically the same—the person passes away and their name is not found in the book of life. *Rev. 21:8, 22:14* These passages say nothing about those who "took the mark", but obviously they would be included in this group. Hmm.

What the mark was, and its threat, existed in some kind of form before the book of Revelation was written. What about the early church in the book of Acts, and the rest of the church through history that were not even aware of the warning not to take the mark of the beast? There must have been some other way that the Spirit warned them about this type of threat.

If the book of Revelation is a message to all of the church, throughout church history, then there must be evidence, or signs of the mark since the day we were warned about it. Whatever it is has to be greater than the UPC code on the back of your cereal box!

There's a lot of fear and discussion about the mark of the beast, and not much talk about the "sealing" of God's servants in other passages in Revelation. *(Rev. 7:4; 14:1)* If the mark of those sealed by God was not something physical, then we should assume rightly that the mark of the beast is not some physical mark either, but it *symbolizes* something *spiritual* instead. Perhaps the mark being on the forehead and the hand simply conveys the idea of not letting the world control how you think and act. *(Rev.13:16)* That's certainly a truth commanded throughout the NT.

**The mark of the beast through the ages**

If one of the main goals of the beast is government control

of the righteous, then you can see it in a number of ways through the centuries. Here are a few:

- The early church through the first three centuries was threatened continually with the worship of the Roman emperors. Many of the emperors considered themselves to be god, and a refusal to acknowledge that came with possible execution, or at the very least, lost economic opportunities in the trade guilds.
- A mid-third century emperor demanded certificates of sacrifice to the emperor to participate in commerce and escape prosecution. Many Christians bribed officials to get the certificates; some others were executed. One could not even handle money without involvement in the imperial system, since the coins regularly bore the emperor's image.
- Later, under papal Rome, thousands were threatened with execution unless they pledged allegiance to the Catholic Church and its many idolatrous practices.
- The various forms of Communism, in the many countries where it is found, requires an allegiance and loyalty to the ruling party.
- Even today, in China, communism requires a strict loyalty to the party line. If you're involved in a church, the communist party only recognizes the "state sponsored church", which is controlled and overseen by the communist party. It is well known that the CCP has developed a "credit score", which it monitors over everybody in order to control them if they get

too out of hand.

- There are many Islamic countries where Jihadist terrorists will gladly execute you rather than tolerate the beliefs of the "infidels". It's convert or die.
- Even one of the greatest mission-sending countries is caving into unbelief and persecuting its own citizens—Great Britain is the current leader of all countries when it comes down to disallowing any kind of negative online posts from its own population.

All of these are examples of different kinds of "marks" that worldly governments want to pin on the righteous, and pressure them into denying the faith. This is why we must use the freedoms we have now, and pray for continued freedom in a greater measure. Pray for evil leaders to repent, or be rooted up and cast out!

As I said early in the book, there are challenges to understanding how all Bible prophecy will be fulfilled. Interpreting the symbolism of the book of Revelation may only make complete sense when history unfolds and we can see how it is *literally* fulfilled. But again, we should be careful in thinking that the book of Revelation mainly applies to the church in the distant future. We need to see its message having application to all of us, whenever we live in history.

This seems to be the intent of heaven when we're told in *Revelation 22:6 "The angel said to me, "These words are trustworthy and true. The Lord, the God of the spirits of the prophets, sent his angel to show his servants the things that* ***must soon*** *take place."*

Indeed, we're already living in the middle of it.

# 13

## OCCUPY UNTIL I COME—WAITING OR WORKING?

**SO MUCH OF** addressing the end times seems to be concerned about fretting over the future, or overlooking the past, and not nearly enough about the present transformation that all of us are called to. *Rom. 12:1–2* In this closing chapter, I want to focus on how we should presently live in light of the Lord's sure return.

As I stated in a previous chapter, Jesus taught that no man knows the hour or the day of His return. The signs of upheaval around us are not nearly sufficient markers to determine his arrival. They may be strong enough to end somebody's world, and influential enough to move people into fear, but God is greater than all of these things and his plan is for us to advance regardless of the difficulties.

None of us can accurately predict the King's return, and nobody really knows how many more generations will pass before the end of all things. So in light of that, we must train on purpose, and be equipped to reach our generation, and prepare future generations to run the next leg of the race, because at some point all of us get replaced!

If we pay close attention to the teachings of Jesus when he came the first time, we can see many indications that there would be a notable amount of time before he would return a second time. Consider some of these statements Jesus made:

*"Then. He said to his disciples, "The time is coming when you will long to see one of the days of the Son of Man, but you will not see it. Men will tell you, "There he is!' Or 'Here he is!' Don't go running off after them. But first he must suffer many things and be rejected by this generation." Luke 17:21–23, 25*

*"He said: A man of noble birth went to a distant country to have himself appointed king and then to return." Luke 19:12*

*"He went on to tell the people this parable: "A man planted a vineyard, rented it to some farmers and went away for a long time." Matt. 20:9*

*"The bridegroom was a long time in coming, and they all became drowsy and fell asleep." Matt. 25:5*

*"After a long time the master of those servants returned and settled accounts with them." Matt. 25:19*

*"You will hear of wars and rumors of wars, but see to it that you are not alarmed. Such things must happen, but the end is still to come. Nation will rise against nation*

*and kingdom against kingdom." Matt. 24:6–7*

Obviously, it takes a lot of time for one nation to rise against another. Nobody wakes up in the morning and says to his friend, "Hey, lets go start a war, are you good with that?"

## THE VALUE OF YOUR LIFE

When you review all of the different kinds of parables Jesus taught you see many different themes, but all of them teach responsible action and efforts on our part. One thing's for sure: laziness, slothfulness, and greed are not kingdom virtues and the work of the Holy Spirit in our lives will purge these out.

Because we don't know the day or the hour of his return it becomes very important to build for the long term, and to realize that all of us only have so much time, talent, and treasure. The following parable is an example of this.

> *"While they were listening to this, he went on to tell them a parable, because he was near Jerusalem and the people thought the kingdom of God was going to appear at once. He said: "A man of noble birth went to a distant country to have himself appointed king and then to return. So he called ten of his servants and gave them ten minas. 'Put this money to work,' he said, 'until I come back.' Luke 19:11–13*

In the above parable of the minas, *(Luke 19:13)*, the mina actually represents quite a large sum. In that day, a mina equaled

100 drachmas, each drachma being worth about a day's wages. The total amount of minas was valued at between two and three years average wages. In this teaching each servant was given the same amount—ten minas apiece, and directed to *"put this money to work until I come back." Luke 19:13*

Although each servant was given the same amount, the return varied from one servant to the other. The first one doubled what was given to him to equal a 100% return. The second one showed much effort as well, and returned to his master a 50% increase. Each of these servants was rewarded by their master with a greater authority and responsibility as well.

This is something we need to see—the King has given us something valuable, and with his grace working on our behalf its designed to bring increase and addition to our life and others. It's not valuable left on its own, but in the light of eternity and touched by the Spirit of God it can be very valuable and influential.

It's a mistake to think that reward and promotion only happens in the next life. The kingdom of God is already here, even if its fullness is still being developed, arriving completely at Jesus' second coming. As the apostle Paul told Timothy, "... *godliness has value for all things, holding promise for both the present life and the life to come." I Tim. 4:8*

## THE PROBLEM WITH THE "KINDERCARE" CHURCH

The church at large is still working its way back to proclaiming the full counsel of God's word, and applying it in every way to fulfill the commission to make disciples in every nation. Unfortunately, too much of the church has a very narrow focus on the depth and breadth of where kingdom principles can be applied. Many church leaders are stuck in a mentality that sees the church primarily as a "soul saving machine", with the major efforts on getting people ready for eternity and making peace with God. This is reaching first base and where it all starts, but it's hardly all that God has for any one of us.

Paul told the church at Ephesus, *"For it is by grace you have been saved, through faith—and this not from yourselves, it is the gift of God—not by works, so that no one can boast. Eph.2:8–9 He went on to tell them that when God is done shaping us, the end result will be far greater, "For we are God's workmanship, created in Christ Jesus to do good works, which God prepared in advance for us to do." Eph. 2:10*

Faith is positioned in a seat called grace, but grace finds its complete fulfillment when we carry out the good works that He has prepared in advance for us to do. Every local church should understand that its ultimate goal is not getting people into the building for the Sunday service, but to equip people to get out of the building and into all the various marketplaces of life to let the light shine and increase the kingdom. In the NT, the "house of the Lord" is not the local church building—it's the people of God themselves. *(II Cor. 6:16)*

As Jesus said, *"You are the light of the world. A city on a hill cannot be hidden. Neither do people light a lamp and put it under a bowl. Instead they put it on its stand and it gives light to everyone in the house. In the same way, let your light shine before men, that they may see your good deeds and praise your Father in heaven." Matt.5:14–16*

It starts with every member of the body of Christ recognizing that they are called to discover, develop, and deploy the gifts and abilities that God has given them. This is not a light matter, or one that is fulfilled in a single season of life. There are no ungifted people in God's kingdom. Only people that are working on discovering who they are in Christ, and what they are capable of doing when they submit their efforts to the direction of God's Spirit. As someone said, without God we cannot do it, and without us He will not do it. A cooperative effort is necessary and even expected.

At the end of our earthly journey, and along the way as well, God desires to show himself to us, not only as our "Great Reward" *(Gen. 15:1)*, but as the rewarder of our efforts as well. Here's a great passage from the book of Hebrews that speaks to this point:

> *"God is not unjust, he will not forget your work and the love you have shown him as you have helped his people and continue to help them. We want you to show this same diligence to the end, in order to make your hope sure. We do not want you to become lazy, but to imitate those who through faith and patience inherit what has been promised." Hebs. 6:10–12*

## YOUR VIEW OF GOD DETERMINES YOUR RESPONSE

Laziness was a big problem for the third servant in the parable of the ten minas. *(Luke 19:20–24)* The fundamental problem was he didn't really understand the character of his master. He had an unhealthy fear of his master, and accused his boss of being difficult to please, and not giving him the necessary abilities to expect the kind of return he was looking for. So, his master told him: *"if that's what you think I'm like, then you should have worked harder to at least get me a little interest back on my money."*

Unfortunately, this is too often the mentality of people when it comes to their view of God. They read the OT and accuse God of being heavy handed and quick to judgment, but they overlook the hundreds of years when he gave people repeated chances to quit their sin.

They pick on the moral failures of others and overlook the grace God extended to people mentioned in the Bible—these people showed faith in God's grace in spite of their performance. They would rather parrot what they've heard about God, than to truly seek him out and find out what He's really like.

Sadly, this is a problem in the church world too, the very place one would hope to see God in a better light. Somehow the overriding theme of the church's teaching seems to be salvation by grace, and perfection by serving in the local church several times a week. You really can't blame some people for not joining. Why would they want to make their life more difficult than it is now?

Many people in God's family are like the older brother in the parable of the prodigal son. *(Luke 15)* When the younger brother repents and returns to the fellowship of the family, the older brother can only look at him with disdain and criticism at the favor the father is showing the younger son. He answers his father with, *"Look! All these years I've been slaving for you and never disobeyed your orders. Yet you never gave me even a young goat so I could celebrate with my friends." Luke 15:29*

Note the shocking reply the father gives his soured son: *'My son,' the father said, you are always with me, and everything I have is yours." Luke 15:31* Do you see what's going on?

One son's conduct cannot keep him from God's grace and

goodness when he remembers it. The other son would rather trust in his conduct and dutiful service to earn the fathers favor, and in the meantime he's completely overlooked the fact that he could've already enjoyed all his father had for him!

In the parable of the ten minas, and the parable of the prodigal son, both men fail to receive God's best because they don't know the character of the one they serve. They've actually put a limit on him. Our understanding of God's character has a much larger part to play in how we live our life than most people think. Even in God's family many do not recognize that God's generosity is available and his kingdom is filled with abundance.

## NOTHING SOWN—NOTHING REAPED

In the parable of the minas, if the third servant had respected the true character of his master, maybe he would have been motivated in a healthy way to use what his master had given him. Instead he buried it and didn't use it at all. Hear the master's response to the servants' neglect: "*Then he said to those standing by, 'Take his mina away from him and give it to the one who has ten minas.' 'Sir,' they said, 'he already has ten!' "He replied, ' I tell you that to everyone who has, more will be given, but as for the one who has nothing, even what he has will be taken away." Luke 19:24–26*

If we fail to live by the principles of the kingdom and engage in initiative and action, our one mina becomes nothing because it was never used. What we fail to value becomes worthless and another will take our position. It's been said in the world of employment, the best person to give a job to is the one that's already busy. If the one with "ten minas" becomes too busy for another task, he's probably already thinking about who he can find to do the job—he's looking to multiply.

This is the kind of kingdom that we live in and the principles we're expected to operate by. A kingdom of action, addition, even multiplication. Yes, Jesus is first of all our Savior, but he is also our king and the master of all his servants, each and every one of us. The words of Jesus inspire initiative, action, and a healthy optimism that growth and change can happen, and the outcome of our efforts gets rewarded.

Some people in the church world think that a Christian government should use other people's money to meet the needs of others who have no ambition to work. Many are counting on somebody else to do the hard work for them. I'm not talking about those who are lame and clearly disabled, I'm talking about those who are capable of pulling their own load. As Thomas Jefferson said, *"A government that is willing to give you everything you want, is powerful enough to take everything you have!"*

Jesus wants us to remember those who are poor indeed, but he never supported the idea that the prosperity of his kingdom would reward everybody equally for unequal efforts.

Again, laziness, slothfulness and greed are not kingdom virtues. The rich man is warned that his life does not consist of what he possesses, but the choice to give still lies within his power and not that of another.

Still, others like to point out that the early church, *"had everything in common. Selling their possessions and goods, they gave to anyone as he had need." Acts 2:44–45* The question naturally follows, isn't this what the church should do? But like all things scriptural, additional counsel is found in other places as well. When Timothy was the overseer at the church at Ephesus, Paul directed him to instruct believers to be the first to take care of their own family members and not let the church carry that burden. *(See I Tim. 5:3–8,16)*

One of the reasons Paul wrote the second letter to the Thessalonians was because they had forgotten the example Paul and his team had set before them—an example of working rather than sitting around waiting for the Lord's return. *"We were not idle when we were with you, nor did we eat anyone's food without paying for it. On the contrary we worked night and day, laboring and toiling so we would not be a burden to any of you." II Thess. 3:7–8* By example, Paul had given them this rule, *"If a man will not work, he shall not eat. We hear that some among you are idle. They are not busy, they are busy bodies. Such people we command and urge in the Lord Jesus Christ to settle down and earn the bread they eat. And as for you brothers, never tire of doing what is right." II Thess. 3:10–13*

Even though the apostle Paul and the other leaders preached like the return of Christ was right around the corner, they knew enough to instruct people to build for the future and to think long term. I like what he instructed Titus to do as another leader in the early church:

> *"Our people must learn to devote themselves to doing what is good, in order that they may provide for daily necessities and not live unproductive lives." Titus 3:14. The NASB stresses the need to be engaged in, "good occupations."*

## WHAT ALL THE PARABLES TEACH US

Besides the many straightforward teachings given by Jesus on how we ought to live, there are at least 40 different parables that all stress responsible action and deeds on our part. These actions are not to earn our salvation, but they are the result of God's grace working out through us the good works he has prepared for us to do. *(Eph. 2:10)*

In regard to the parables most closely connected to his return, here's seven observations that can help us live out our salvation, and prepare for his second coming.

1. God's grace is extended for a really long time. When Jesus said his return was like the *"master returning after a long time"*, He wasn't kidding!

2. God owns everything and has ultimate control over everybody, even those who do not acknowledge his name. An example of this would be the death of Christ. *Acts 2:23 says, "This man was handed over to you by God's set purpose and foreknowledge; and you, with the help of wicked men, put him to death by nailing him to the cross."* God foresaw the decisions that men would make and he worked within those decisions to act on our behalf. What was terribly evil worked out for our eternal good.

   Other historical examples would be men like Pharaoh, Nebuchadnezzar & Cyrus.

3. Everybody is called to be equipped by

discovering, developing, and deploying what God has given them. The gifting, the function, and the capacity will differ from one person to another. Just like the human body functions with a diversity of organs, a healthy society requires a diversity of functions and gifts as well.

4. Using what we have faithfully will bring increase and favor for more. The classic example of this is seen in the life of Joseph. *(See Gen. 37)* It wasn't easy but God brought it to pass. Even though Joseph did not know how or when it would take place, he stayed faithful.

5. God desires to reward us and advance us because we're joint heirs with Christ. This is seen in countless stories in the Bible and stated repeatedly by the words of Christ.

6. Some people squander future opportunities by not using what they've been given.

   (*We'll look at this closer shortly)*

7. Everyone born on earth is designed to be a contributing member of society, whether they acknowledge the Creator or not. God is the final judge over every life.

When we get to the book of Revelation, and look at the

letters Jesus commissioned John to send to the seven churches, it shouldn't surprise us that we would hear echoes of the parables that Christ taught during his earthly ministry. In his resurrected state, Jesus, the Head of the church, is seen walking through the seven churches and observing the progress they had made—individually and corporately. Some had done quite well, and others needed some "adjustment" shall we say. *(See Rev. 2 & 3)*

## WHEN THE MASTER SPEAKS

All of these churches faced great tribulation in their day, and it was a temptation to cave into the world around them, but Jesus was aware of the storms they faced, and just like he came walking on the water when the disciples were sinking in the storm, he now came walking through the churches to remind them that He is our goal and the true source of victory.

The churches were made up of people just like you and me that had goals, desires, challenges and sorrows. Each of them were promised a great reward for overcoming the tests they faced. Several times Christ said such phrases as: *"I will give … I will grant … I will reward"*. Christ knew they could overcome and just like a good coach he talked to them like they already had won. As the apostle John said in an earlier letter:

*"For everyone born of God overcomes the world. This is the victory that has overcome the world, even our faith. Who is it that overcomes the world? Only he who believes that Jesus is the Son of God." I John 5:4–5*

## GROWING PAINS

Let's not hide the fact that not everybody is interested in growing up. That's evident from the parables Jesus taught and from the observations of church life, both in the Bible and around us. Growing up spiritually may not be easy but it is God's goal for all of us. Certainly our conduct, our attitudes, and our motives all play a part in this. We discover its important to do the right thing for the right reasons.

An example of this is when Jesus pointed out that the Pharisees did many spiritual looking things, such as fasting and praying loudly just to be seen by others. If that was their motive, then when others saw them that was also their reward and the only one they got. *(Matt. 6:5)*

If we've neglected to grow up when we've had plenty of opportunities to do so, Paul says it is like trying to build on a foundation with wood, hay, or straw. It won't last forever, it'll all get burned up—in other words it will not be rewarded. The good news is that this judgment has nothing to do with the loss of salvation, and everything to do with the hope of reward. It's an accounting of the stewardship of what God has given us, and the use of our gifts and resources during our earthly life. *(See I Cor. 3:11–15)*

The apostle Paul lived very aware of this and shared his convictions when he told the Corinthians: *"Do you not know that in a race all the runners run, but only one gets the prize? Run in such a way as to get the prize. Everyone who competes in the games goes into strict training. They do it to get a crown that will last forever. Therefore I do not run like a man running aimlessly; I do not fight like a man beating the air. No, I beat my body and make it my slave so that after I have preached to others, I myself will not be disqualified for the prize." I Cor. 9:24–27*

## WHAT KIND OF DEEDS GET REWARDED?

*"What good is it my brothers, if a man claims to have faith but has no deeds? Can such faith save him? James 2:14* Probably not. In the mind of the NT writers, all of them expected some kind of obvious fruit to accompany the lives of those who made up the church community. Fruit takes time to develop but as new creations in Christ we're designed to produce lasting fruit when we remain in fellowship with Christ. *(John 15:4–5)*

When the apostle John writes to the church, he provides them with a simple test to see if somebody is a true believer or a religious phony. In *I John 3:14–15* John says, *"We know that we have passed from death to life, because we love our brothers. Anyone who does not love remains in death. Anyone who hates his brother is a murderer, and you know that no murderer has eternal life in him."*

The thief on the cross that hung next to Christ was promised eternal life moments before he died. He had not done any deeds that showed he had real faith, but he's a great example of the truth that we are saved by faith in the grace of God alone. Had he continued to live and been a part of the congregation that James led, he would be expected to complete his faith by adding deeds to it.

Using Abraham as an example, he points out that Abraham was justified by God and credited with righteousness when he believed the offer God gave. *(Gen. 15:3)* That was the start of a true heart felt faith. James uses a later time in Abraham's life when he was willing to offer up Issac as a sacrifice to give us an example of works following faith. *(James 2:20–21)* He goes on to say,

> *"You see that his faith and his actions were **working together**, and his faith was **made complete** by what he did". James 2:22*

> *"You see that a person is justified by what he does and not by faith alone." James 2:24*

Faith and works are like the two sides of the same coin. Faith in God's grace represents the head of the coin and that comes first. Works, or deeds, are the tail side of the coin and that comes after faith. Trying to save ourselves by faith in our own works is called "dead works" in many places of Scripture, and we're commanded to turn from dead works, and turn in faith toward God. *(Hebs. 6:2)*

If we stay rooted in Christ and walk in fellowship with him, we will be challenged regarding what we think, say, and do. God is not impossible to please and he simply expects a measurable amount of progress in a reasonable amount of time. It's understood that a baby will wet their diaper at six months of age, but a wet diaper on a sixteen year old indicates a larger problem. Are you with me?

So, what are these good deeds that we're supposed to carry out? What do they look like?

> Is it selling everything you have and moving to a foreign country to live in discomfort?

> Is it preaching a giant crusade with hundreds of sinners

raising their hands for salvation?

Is it inventing a cutting edge technology that changes the economic world?

Is it building a Fortune 500 company that appears on the front cover of *Forbes* magazine?

Is it being one of the "stars" and celebrities on the walk of fame?

It possibly *could* include that if you're gifted that way and have that capacity, but of course you won't get there on your own, because it will require lots of people behind the curtain; the "unknowns", doing all the little things that many people never see. But Jesus sees it—just like he saw the deeds of the members of the seven churches in Revelation.

It's noteworthy that several people who carried out good deeds, did so in the context of everyday events that at times seem mundane, common, and perhaps boring. In NT times widows were often marginalized and faced difficulties, but a widow could be, *"well known for her good deeds, such as bringing up children, showing hospitality, washing the feet of the saints, helping those in trouble and devoting herself to all kinds of good deeds." I Tim. 5:9–10*

*"All kinds of good deeds"*—well, that could be a growing list. Cornelius, the Roman commander, was a man who gave generously to those in need and prayed to God regularly. So much that his deeds rose as a memorial offering to God. *Acts 10:2–4*

A lady named Dorcas was well known as a seamstress, *"who was always doing good and helping the poor." Acts 9:36*

Paul counseled Timothy to, *"Command those who are rich in*

*this present world not to be arrogant nor to put their hope in wealth … but to do good, to be rich in good deeds, and to be generous and willing to share. In this way they will lay up treasure for themselves as a firm foundation for the coming age, so they may take hold of the life that is truly life." I Timothy 6:17,18–19*

Even something as small as a cup of cold water to a truly thirsty disciple has the potential to be rewarded. Jesus said in *Matt. 10:42 "And if anyone gives even a cup of cold water to one of these little ones because he is my disciple, I tell you the truth, he will certainly not lose his reward."*

When you consider much of the direction from the NT, it would seem that our best deeds are when we want to serve others simply because it's an expression of God's love, and we have no other motive—we just want to help and be a blessing to somebody.

The background for living a life of good deeds comes from the teachings of Jesus, and the example he showed us repeatedly with his life, like washing the disciples feet after hours of trudging along dusty roads. Or, reaching out to the lowlifes and downcasts in society, instead of cultivating an audience with the rich and influential.

> *"One Sabbath, Jesus went to eat in the house of a prominent Pharisee, … he noticed how the guests picked the places of honor at the table, so he told them a parable". Luke 14:1,7*

At the end of the parable he said plainly to his host:

> *"When you give a luncheon or dinner, do not invite your*

*friends, your brothers, or relatives, or your rich neighbors; if you do, they may invite you back and so you will be repaid. But when you give a banquet, invite the poor, the crippled, the lame, the blind, and you will be blessed. Although they cannot repay you, you will be repaid at the resurrection of the righteous." Luke 14:12–14*

Besides the obvious point here, I think the spirit of this teaching reminds us that Christ has died for all kinds of people, and even if they are not physically poor and crippled, if they are without Christ, they are definitely spiritually poor and broken. And they're worthy of us taking our time, talent, and money to reach out to them, even if they can never repay us in this life. When you know God is your provider and reward it takes the pressure off you from trying to, "close the deal", and make the sale with everybody that appears to be a friend.

## JESUS IS SOMEWHERE IN THE CROWD

The impact of what Jesus taught that day is seen again when he points out the existing conditions at his return in *Matt. 25:31.* Here, he reveals what a life of service that looks like—its being open to opportunities to help those less fortunate, especially those that can never repay us in this life.

*"Then the righteous will answer him, 'Lord, when did we see you hungry and feed you, or thirsty and give you something to drink? When did we see you as a stranger and invite you in, or needing clothes and clothe you?*

*When did we see you sick or in prison and go to visit you?*

*The King will reply, 'I tell you the truth, whatever you did for one of the least of these brothers of mine, you did for me.' " Matt. 25:37–40*

When we live a life of service like that, it's not only a picture of the care we should show for others in the body of Christ, it's a picture of the same grace Jesus showed us when he gave us the fullness of his life, knowing there is no way we could ever pay him back for the great love he has shown us.

God takes care of his servants, and some day it will be such an encouraging word to hear, *"Well done good and faithful servant." Matt. 25:23*

Likewise, we're told in the book of *Revelation 14:13: "Then I heard a voice from heaven say, "Write: Blessed are the dead who die in the Lord from now on." "Yes." says the Spirit, "they will rest from their labor, for their deeds will follow them."*

## INVESTING YOUR TIME, TALENT, & TREASURE

In this chapter we've been considering the importance of faithfully using what God has placed in our hands. Because we don't know the hour or day of his return, each of us must think long term and consider that others will follow after us, should Jesus not return in our lifetime. A balanced life takes this into consideration and so does the Bible. God chose Abraham, Issac, and Jacob as carriers of the same vision that took over 400 years to complete. Each one of them was a part of the full picture

God had in mind.

We must think the same way. Our lives have a "shelf life", and an "expiration date" if you will, that we have to consider. In the next life we are not limited by time, we're not in need of treasure, and there is no wasted talent. In this life we face limitations, however, we can extend our time, talent, and treasure by what we deposit into others within our sphere of influence.

Here are some lines of thought to reflect on, and some questions to ask yourself regarding the time, talent, and treasure you have.

**Have you taken the time to invest in yourself *spiritually*?**

*Nothing* is more important than your relationship with God, and it has *everything* to do with how you relate to others. When you're at peace with God, you become a peacemaker.

**Who can you influence with your time and talent?**

It might be a child, grandchild, niece or nephew, an old friend, a business associate, an intern, apprentice, a student, maybe a neighbor, etc. Somebody's in your circle of influence.

**Have you discovered your talents, and abilities and gifts that best suit you?**

**Are you using them and developing them to influence others?**

***Some key markers:***

> It comes easy for you and others think you're a "natural" at it.
>
> It gets you energized and motivated in a healthy way, perhaps even stirred up.
>
> You would do it if you never made a dollar from it.

You take the time to improve yourself at it.

You're willing to give it away to others because you see the value of it.

**Have you extended your money and treasure to meet the needs of others, and not just yourself? Is any of your money given to causes and people that can never repay you?**

It's not about equal giving—it's about equal sacrifice—*Luke 21:1–4*.

Money is an influential tool and when used rightly, it can help others and "go ahead of us" into eternity—Luke 16:9–*12*.

Look for safe investments that can increase and outlive you to be a blessing to others.

Look for those in your circle of influence that can catch the vision of generosity to others.

# APPENDIX

## CHAPTER 3

26 **Note 1** Roger Mullan, **earthquakes.bgs.ac.uk**

26 **Note 2** **answers.usgs.gov**

## CHAPTER 4

34 **Note 1** Rather than reinvent the wheel, I would recommend *Four Views of the End Times*, published by Rose Publishing. This is a laminated fold out chart, with a complete summary, provided in a condensed form, with everything you need. Available online.

## CHAPTER 5

41 **Note 1** Josephus, *Wars of the Jews,* Volume II.15–19

42 **Note 2** Eusebius, *Ecclesiastical History*, Book III.5

42 **Note 3** Josephus, *Wars of the Jews*, Volume VI.9.3–4

## CHAPTER 6

54 **Note 1** Dating the time of the birth of Christ—a mistake in dating arose in 532 A.D. when Dionysius Exiguus invented the calendar of the Christian era based upon the building of the city of Rome. This kind of time was called urbe condita, or U.C. time. Dionysius placed the birth of Christ in 753 U.C. Later when it was determined that Herod had died in 750, Jesus' birth was moved back to the latter part of 749 U.C., a little more than three years before 1 A.D. Therefore Christ was 30 years of age in 27 A.D. See Luke 3:23. Remember to count the zero years as well.

## CHAPTER 8

87 **Note 1** Schwarz, *Handbook of the Christian Faith*, p. 150

87 **Note 2** Schwarz, *Handbook of the Christian Faith,* p. 153

88 **Note 3** Schwarz, *Handbook of the Christian Faith,* p. 153

88 **Note 4** Schwarz, *Handbook of the Christian Faith,* pp. 154–155 The author does a good job of separating the primary differences between the two groups. He also covers the Crusade period of 1095–1291 and explains the failure of those trips.

## CHAPTER 10

131 **Note 1** Halley, *Halley's Bible Handbook*, p. 763.

131 **Note 2** Halley, *Halley's Bible Handbook*, pp. 776–777, 785

131 **Note 3** Williams-Ayedun, "I'm a Christian from Niger. Don't Ignore Horrifying Attacks on African Christians," *Fox News*, Oct. 26, 2025

## CHAPTER 11

150 **Note 1** Brown & Keener, *Not Afraid of the Antichrist*, pp. 196–98

150 **Note 2** Brown & Keener, *Not Afraid of the Antichrist*, pp. 196–198

151 **Note 3** Brown & Keener, *Not Afraid of the Antichrist*, pp. 196–198

159 **Note 4** Hagin, *The Believer's Authority* (Legacy Edition), p. 104

# ALSO PUBLISHED BY

## PAUL FREDERICK DWYER

**TOWARD GREATER GROWTH**
12 Essential Pillars for Successful Spiritual Growth

www.ingramcontent.com/pod-product-compliance
Lightning Source LLC
LaVergne TN
LVHW010657110826
845149LV00014B/3134

*9798994745205*